Computers in the Information Society

Nathan Weinberg

CALIFORNIA STATE UNIVERSITY–NORTHRIDGE

Westview Press

BOULDER, SAN FRANCISCO, & OXFORD

Copyright © 1990 by Westview Press, Inc.

Published in 1990 in the United States of America by Westview Press, Inc., 5500 Central Avenue, Boulder, Colorado 80301, and in the United Kingdom by Westview Press, Inc., 36 Lonsdale Road, Summertown, Oxford OX2 7EW

Library of Congress Cataloging-in-Publication Data
Weinberg, Nathan.
 Computers in the information society / Nathan Weinberg.
  p. cm.
 Includes bibliographical references.
 ISBN 0-8133-0986-7 (alk. paper). — ISBN 0-8133-0985-9 (pbk. : alk. paper)
 1. Computers and civilization. I. Title.
QA76.9.C66W45 1990
303.48′34—dc20

90-11981
CIP

Printed and bound in the United States of America

The paper used in this publication meets the requirements of the American National Standard for Permanence of Paper for Printed Library Materials Z39.48-1984.

10 9 8 7 6 5 4 3 2 1

To Chessa and Zachary

Contents

Tables

Acknowledgments

Several years ago when I was thinking about the increasing role of personal computers in our lives and considering how I might write about it, my friend Ronald Schwartz, of the Sociology Department at Memorial University, St. John's, Newfoundland, made one of his summer visits to California. During his stay, we found we thought along similar lines about the ways computers were becoming a part of our world, and we decided to collaborate on a book. I started to work on the history of computers and Ron returned to Newfoundland and started on the subject of artificial intelligence. If we had known how arduous this type of book would be, we might never have attempted it. Over the next three years, we exchanged ideas and explored the rapidly changing role of computers. Ron prepared a draft of the chapter on artificial intelligence but decided not to continue with the book when he went on an extended sabbatical to Asia to pursue his research in Tibet. For his friendship, his comments on the early chapters, and the enthusiasm he brought to our work, I owe him a debt of gratitude.

The first chapters of the book were written on an Osborne 1 computer with 64K memory using WordStar software and the CPM operating system. Later chapters were prepared on a Macintosh computer with 128K memory (soon expanded to 512K). The final revision was completed on a Macintosh Plus with 1MB of memory. In many ways, my personal experience and occasional frustration with these machines has become a part of this book. I am sure many other computer users have shared similar experiences over the last decade.

Many colleagues and friends at California State University at Northridge encouraged and supported my research on this book. I thank John Motil, Diane Schwartz, and Rein Turn of the Computer Science Department; Earl Bogdanoff, John Crowther, and Harvey Rich of the Sociology Department; and Chris Sales and Larry Wake of the Computer Center. In many conversations, they provided valuable insights into the ways computers are changing the university and other institutions. I also thank Michael Devirian for his observations on NASA data systems, and Anthony Bernhard and Richard Farrell for their comments on computers.

As the book has progressed, I have received editorial support from John Sulzycki, John Stout, and Dean Birkenkamp. I was assisted in the final preparation of the book for publication by Deborah Lynes and Anna M. Huff. I thank all for their assistance.

I also thank my wife, Virginia, for the help she gave me in editing the manuscript, and my children, Zachary and Chessa, for the patience they have shown during the many hours I spent at the computer.

Nathan Weinberg
Woodland Hills, California

Introduction

Prior to 1980, computers and information systems were powerful but unfamiliar parts of the technology of our society. With the personal computer revolution, they became familiar if not commonplace. Ready access to computers and information databases has completely altered our relationship to this technology and has laid the foundation for the information society.

Computers, either alone or linked in networks, are changing the way in which people learn, work, and communicate. In this book we examine the unfolding cultural and organizational impact of computers on our society. Through this analysis we will come to better understand the role of information technology in our everyday and professional lives and the increasing interdependence between human society and its computer creations.

Through computers and information networks, human knowledge is becoming available at all points in society—whether to the individual, the school, the corporation, or the state. Using this information we can monitor, simulate, and control the processes of the physical, economic, and social worlds. In many respects, the information society can reach the scientific goal of understanding and controlling our environment.

Developing on an infrastructure of computers integrated with communications networks, the information society is not fixed in its form or structure. In the first decades of computerization, mainframe computer centers and time-sharing networks were the institutional norms, and large-scale data processing applications were the usual computational tasks. Since 1980, the focus of computing has shifted to mini- and microcomputer installations, local networks, and personalized applications. The end user requires a flexible and friendly computing environment that links micro and mainframe computer resources in a seamless and transparent network. This is the new computer environment that manufacturers and designers are working to create.

In society generally, computers and information systems are causing substantial changes. However, as in any social transformation, the use of computers is not proceeding at the same pace in all areas, nor are the benefits of information technology evenly distributed. Some institutions have moved rapidly ahead, others have lagged behind. Problems and obstacles lie in the path of change to the information society. The investment cost in computer hardware and software is one major obstacle. The retraining of workers in organizations and factories is another. Nevertheless, in the United States, Japan, and Europe the governments and major institutions have committed themselves to this change as a necessary element for maintaining their economic, political, and military positions in the next century.

The text begins with an introduction to the role of technology in social change and a consideration of the expectations for computers and communications in the information society. The second chapter takes up the history of computer technology and begins our discussion of the organizational framework surrounding the use of computers. The following chapters on the computer culture and the computer in organizations describe the cultural and institutional frameworks that have developed over the last four decades and explore the differences that exist in the mainframe and personal computer environments. This portion of the book presents a coherent view of the technical, cultural, and organizational changes that have come with the widespread use of information processing technologies.

The next four chapters move from the overall picture to the specific effects of computers in education, government, health care, and industry. New goals and ways of working with computers are emerging in each of these social arenas, and a new culture is being formed using computers for analysis and distribution of information and for monitoring and control of technical processes. In education, the computer is changing the learning environment in the home, the school, and the university. In government, the computer is essential for the collection of social data and for everyday government operations. At the same time, government data banks may pose a threat to our privacy and liberty. In medicine, computer analyses and monitoring are changing the nature of patient care and altering the operation of hospitals. In diagnosis and health care delivery, the computer is becoming the constant assistant of the health care specialist. In industry, the techniques of factory automation, computer machine programming, and robotics are transforming or superseding the techniques of traditional manufacturing. We will examine the Japanese model of production, management and labor problems, and other issues in factory automation.

The final portion of the book looks at the future of computers and society. The chapter on artificial intelligence examines human and machine intelligence and reviews the efforts to create intelligence in computers. In the last chapter, the themes of cultural and organizational change and the positive and negative aspects of computerization are summarized. Some computer enthusiasts expect that the information society will usher in a human utopia. However, other writers are skeptical about these utopian expectations and critical of the coming of the information society. Computers and information networks could easily be used to extend the state's control over the individual and the group. In the workplace, the computer can displace, monitor, or speed workers in their tasks. With artificial intelligence, computer decision making could displace human control. The potential autonomy of intelligent computers raises a new set of concerns.

In the last decade, the new information environment has developed as computers and microprocessors entered the social and institutional mainstreams. Although there is widespread awareness of the changes coming with computers, most analyses proceed piecemeal from one topic to the next. By analysing the changing contexts in which computers are used we are able to see how the values and goals of science and industry are transformed. This perspective provides a view of computers and information technology that is consistent with our understanding of the development of science and industry and that looks forward to the emerging information environment.

Technology, Computers, and Society

The rapid development of computer and microchip technology in the last forty years and particularly in the last decade has been revolutionary in ways we are only beginning to understand. The miniaturization of electronic circuitry has made possible computers with ever more power and memory at lower cost. With X-ray lithography and new microchip design architectures, miniaturization will continue to advance to at least the end of the century. Yet, even as we approach the limit of existing lithographic techniques used to draw the chip circuitry, experimental techniques, including optical and biological circuits, are being developed to allow higher circuit densities. We can reasonably expect computers to increase in processing power and memory in the foreseeable future.

Even without further miniaturization, the latest personal computers and workstations are more powerful than existing software applications can readily use. As processing power and memory increase, software and hardware will be tailored to more specific purposes. In a brief time, we have become accustomed to the presence of computers in our homes, schools, and offices. In one respect, this development represents the latest stage of the industrial revolution. In another regard, computers are part of an electronic revolution leading toward a new society—an information society dependent on computer processing and mass data storage. From both perspectives, computers and microprocessors have become the technology defining and delimiting many of the changes in our world.

The Industrial Society

The modern world that surrounds us is the outcome of four centuries of social and technological change. The industrial revolution began in societies that were predominantly rural and agrarian. Systems of manufacturing arose from innovations in commerce and production and gradually changed the agrarian world into the mechanized urban environment that we inhabit. The pace of commerce grew in the seventeenth and eighteenth centuries with major European ports handling imported raw materials from Asia and America and shipping out European commodities. This world system of raw-material import and finished-good export marked the demise of small-scale craft manufacture and local trade. In the nineteenth century, scientific discoveries and inventions led to dramatic improvements in technology and the scale of production.

The transition from the traditional agrarian society to the industrial society was not smooth. Political and social strife was commonplace, and many groups opposed the disruption of the agrarian and craft world. Only in the twentieth century have we come generally to accept social and economic change. Cultural values and beliefs that welcome new technologies have achieved widespread approval. Among these are

1. belief in the effectiveness of technology and science to resolve problems and bring about progress,
2. enthusiastic reception of new inventions in the home and workplace,
3. willingness to try new modes of working and organization in industry and in society generally, and
4. acceptance of new ways of thinking, learning, and communicating.

In the industrial society, the values of the new, the modern, and the efficient have gradually replaced older values. At times, the advent of a post-industrial society in which leisure and sports would take on a new importance has seemed imminent.

The fully developed industrial society of this century rests upon a complex technological infrastructure of information, procedure, and organization. This infrastructure is characterized by

1. large-scale organization for supply, production, and exchange of commodities,
2. application of technical/scientific rationality to all problems and processes,
3. institutional administrative centralization and record keeping, and

4. increasing specialization and interdependence in all spheres of activity (education, labor, manufacture, and service).

The advanced industrial system rests upon a global pattern of communication, finance, manufacture, and trade that links the most technologically developed societies with less developed societies. Few societies have been able to resist the attractions of technological advance.

The development and wide adoption of computers and microprocessors marks a new technological plateau and has led to a new set of expectations for the near future of industrial society.

1. Industrial work will be largely automated through the use of robots.
2. New industries and services based on computers and communication will flourish.
3. A new decentralized pattern of work at home on computers will emerge.
4. New forms of organization based on computers and communication will develop.

These expectations are not far removed from the vision of the post-industrial society. At the same time, computers accelerate the existing tendencies in the technological structure toward centralization and control, interdependence, specialization, and application of scientific/ technical rationality.

In the recent past, industrial society has received wireless radio, airplanes, television, nuclear power, satellites, and many other inventions with great expectations of marvelous change. Although we may greet new inventions with enthusiasm, the widespread adoption of a new technology is a complex cultural and organizational task. In the long term, we can see considerable change in the technological structure of society from the accumulated impact of many inventions and scientific breakthroughs. Social and cultural changes are more difficult to assess. In the case of any particular new invention or breakthrough, the expectation of revolutionary change may prove to be exaggerated. We have only recently learned to study and assess the impact of new technologies as we deploy them. The damage from environmental pollution and technological disasters have forced us to evaluate the balance of positive and negative effects from technological change.

The Telephone and Society—A Case Study

Interesting parallels exist between the development of the telephone system over the last century and what is taking place today with computers. We can gain some perspective on our expectations for computers by considering the expectations for telephones and the actual system that emerged. The introduction of workable telephones after the Bell inventions of the 1870s produced a large volume of predictions and speculations about the uses and social consequences of telephones. These predictions have been analyzed by Ithiel de Sola Pool in *Forecasting the Telephone: A Retrospective Technology Assessment.* He divided the forecasts into twelve groups including predictions for telephone system development and services; impacts on the city, environment, economy, and polity; impacts on social organization and customs; and impacts on conceptions of self and culture. Within each group, forecasts were categorized as

- Type A—the telephone will be used in manner x
- Type B—the telephone will be used in manner x, so society will be changed in manner y
- Type C—with wide use of phones, society will be changed in manner y
- Type D—other propositions[1]

The same categories could easily be applied to a study of forecasts about the computer.

We cannot review all the predictions about the impact of the telephone, but some relate directly to current predictions for computers. For example, consider the following forecasts:

1. Telephones will become pervasive and universal.
2. The telephone system will require directories and phonograph records will be used as a storage medium.
3. Telephones will foster the separation of plant and office and favor the growth of skyscrapers, suburbs, and urban sprawl.
4. Telephones will end rural isolation; the rural operator provides many community services.
5. Telephones will democratize hierarchic relations and foster management from a distance.
6. Telephones will open new job opportunities but messenger jobs will decline.
7. Telephones will be used for shopping.
8. Telephones will increase productivity.

9. Telephones will foster government growth but reduce bureaucratic rigidity and the keeping of written records.
10. Telephones will be useful for reaching voters and will democratize society.
11. International telephony will foster world peace.
12. Telephones will be useful for command and control in warfare.
13. Telephones will improve law enforcement but telephone crime will be a problem.
14. Use of the telephone will reduce the need to travel and provide a bond for communities.
15. Codes of telephone courtesy will develop.
16. Telephones will both increase and decrease privacy and foster both sociability and impersonality.
17. Telephones will facilitate dissemination of knowledge.
18. Telephones will change people's sense of distance.

These forecasts, both positive and negative, reflect the varied effects of the telephone on different parts of communities and institutions. Some impacts are contradictory. The telephone does increase and decrease privacy; it does foster sociability and impersonality; and it is used by world leaders to communicate and by armies to direct the troops. Many of the changes associated with the telephone were also characteristic of the industrial system as it developed. However, as the example of the Soviet Union shows, the telephone system could have been very different.

> Phone books are not made generally available, so unless one knows a person's number one can call only by using directory assistance, and many important numbers are not given out. The system, therefore, becomes to a great degree one of group communication within closed circles. That philosophy is further expressed in the existence of several segregated telephone networks for different institutions. The most significant is the "key" system which links members of the top elite, and which can only be dialed by someone with a key to unlock the instrument. In the Soviet Union the total of phones on the several segregated networks is apparently greater than that of the public network.[2]

Our assumptions that telephones and directories would be widely available and that telephones would enhance democracy and the free exchange of information were facets of our culture more than of the technology itself. Yet at the same time, for reasons of privacy and security many U.S. telephone numbers are unlisted and many institutions have private internal directories and central exchanges to control entry.

The advantage that may be gained from access to persons or information leads us to sequester and hoard these resources. For computers as much as telephones, demands for information privacy and security may intrinsically be at odds with unrestricted access and free flow of information. It is not a simple task to separate the changes inherent in a new technology from the cultural meanings and restrictions that attach to that technology when it is put to use in a society.

In the above list of forecasts, the computer could easily be substituted for the telephone. This is not a coincidence, as the telephone and the computer can serve similar communication functions. Although a complete phone system was in place in the United States by 1940, many new possibilities for the network have emerged with computers and satellites. The idea of a comprehensive telecommunications system has altered our conception of the telephone as an instrument. A telecommunications network was not imagined when the telephone was introduced, but there was some consideration of the new telephone network's relationship to the existing telegraph network.

In *Online Communities,* a study of computer conferences in the office environment, Starr Hiltz has found that new media of communication can either substitute for, add on to, or expand older forms. In the case of the telephone and the telegraph in the United States, the telephone was substituted for the telegraph; in Europe, the two systems coexisted and the telephone system was not as extensive as in the United States. More recently, however, as increasing amounts of text, data, and pictures are transmitted over telephone lines by computers and fax machines, the telephone and telegraph functions are merging in a single system. This was predicted when the telephone was introduced but was impeded for almost a century in our society by the institutional and regulatory separation of the two modes of communication. With the break-up of the AT&T system, the United States is taking a free market course to telecommunications integration. In France, on the other hand, the merging of telegraph, telephone, and teletext networks is proceeding under government sponsorship.

The Telephone Culture

When new inventions are put to use, a unique culture often develops around them. As the telephone came into widespread use a distinctive telephone culture was created. The role of the operator as a source of aid and information in the placing of calls was of great significance. From assisting and eavesdropping on many calls, the local operator became a source for community gossip. The development of automatic switching and telephone directories has gradually limited this interesting role. In the computer culture, the computer bulletin board operator has a similar role.

Another part of telephone culture centers on the etiquette and privacy surrounding telephone conversations. The rules that dictate who can and cannot listen to a call range from customary, though often violated, injunctions not to listen to personal conversations to court-sanctioned regulations governing wiretaps. In early telephone systems, several customers shared the same line and listening in on conversations was not uncommon. With the demise of the shared line we have come to expect telephone privacy; however, children and teenagers often eavesdrop on extension phones. The regulations surrounding wiretap information and its use in criminal proceedings have been subjects of extensive litigation in the courts. Law enforcement agencies continue to press for more extensive wiretap authority. The underlying issue of what constitutes private information and who has access to it reappears in the controversy about computers and privacy.

A telephone conversation can create a unique sense of intimacy and immediacy. The lengthy and frequent telephone conversations of teenagers are one example; pay-per-call adult fantasy services are another. In *Understanding Media,* Marshall McLuhan saw the telephone as an instrument working against rigid communication hierarchies: "One of the most startling consequences of the telephone was its introduction of a 'seamless web' of interlaced patterns in management and decision making. It is not feasible to exercise delegated authority by telephone. The pyramidal structure of job-division and description and delegated powers cannot withstand the speed of the phone to bypass all hierarchical arrangements, and to involve people in depth."[3] To avoid the intrusion and immediate demand of a telephone call, we have invented the unlisted number and the automatic answering machine. Receptionists and secretaries are often used to screen calls. Once caught on the phone, etiquette prevents many of us from hanging up on persistent salespeople or polite strangers. It may even prove difficult to hang up on the talking salescomputer. In the computer culture, electronic mail, conferences, and bulletin boards produce this unique sense of involvement and open new arenas for communication and self-expression.

The Telephone and Social Organization

The technical and organizational problems encountered and resolved in the establishment of the first national telephone networks—problems of equipment standardization and compatibility, line placement, and overlap of service areas—are generic problems faced in setting up networks. For example, such problems exist when setting up local-area and wide-area networks for computers. In the United States, the problem of independent telephone companies that isolated their customers from competing networks was overcome through the establishment of the national Bell network. However, the near monopoly enjoyed by the Bell companies was politically controversial, and regulations were formulated that effectively restricted the extension of the network to include the telegraph and, later, other communication media. As a result, different networks were developed for the telephone, radio, television, and cable systems.

The data transmission needs of computers have imposed new demands on these systems. To handle the increasing load of voice and data transmissions, communications companies are replacing low-capacity analog networks with high-capacity digital fiber-optic networks. The new telephone networks have the potential to simultaneously carry voice, data, video, videotext, and fax and to provide services like call forwarding, call screening, and conference calls. The extension of fiber-optic links to offices and homes in the next decade will make it possible to deliver a variety of communications services over a single network. We are also building high-capacity computer networks region by region, and the government is considering the establishment of a national backbone network for computers. It is anticipated that the telephone and computer networks, sharing common communication protocols, will come to comprise an integrated high-speed network.

The introduction and use of telephones involved a complex of technical and cultural innovations. Our perception and use of an invention like the telephone or the computer are conditioned by prevailing attitudes toward change, innovation, and communication. In modern democratic societies, which value innovation, we receive inventions positively and quickly adapt them to many uses. In more traditional or authoritarian societies, the use of an invention is limited by concern for the social disruption that may be occasioned by new modes of working, thinking, and communicating. Even in advanced societies, the uses of new inventions are restricted by existing institutional arrangements, budgetary considerations, and social pressures to maintain the status quo. Despite the positive value placed on innovation, the force of technological advance does not sweep everything before it.

Computers, Communications, and the Information Society

In the emerging information society, telecommunication and computer networks will be integrated, producing a communications system accessible from any point on the planet. In France, Simon Nora and Alain Minc found in a report to the government that a two-directional, digital, high-capacity network offering comprehensive services is replacing the discrete communications networks. This "telematic" network overcomes the technical differences and division of services found among the existing analog and digital networks. In Japan, Koji Kobayashi, the president of electronics conglomerate NEC, foresees the convergence of computers and communications creating a multilayered structure of information accessible from home or office. U.S. futurists John Naisbitt and Alvin Toffler share similar visions of an impending global communications system, and AT&T has begun to advertise a "global telecommunity."

The observations upon which these European, Japanese, and U.S. visions are based assume a straightforward development of current technologies. Over the next decades, we expect that steady improvements will be made in communications networks and in computer capacity and accessibility to the user. The specialized knowledge currently required to use computers will decrease. With the network integration of computers and communications, the information for analysis, planning, problem solving, and control will be readily available in institutional, corporate, and home environments. Through the global communications infrastructure, information data banks and services will be accessible from either near or remote locations.

As the information society develops, some express concern about the social dislocations that are accompanying computerization. On the global scale, some societies are information rich, others information poor. The control the developed world exerts over the new technology seems to perpetuate existing inequalities of wealth and power. Labor cost savings achieved through automation threaten to reverse the labor cost advantage enjoyed by many developing countries. Rather than narrowing the gaps between the advanced nations, the developing nations, and the poor nations, the new technology may actually widen them.

Within the advanced societies, similar questions of wealth and status, power and control, and work and unemployment surround the introduction of the new technology. Management and labor view the benefits of information processing very differently. For managers, computers offer new vistas of centralization and control in the office and the factory. For workers, computers threaten a loss of skills and potential loss of work. In the rush to embrace the information society, we should not gloss over the concerns of those who work in the automated factories and offices.

In line with other advanced industrial technologies, the computer is redefining social relations in the workplace. Alongside the questions of power and status that surround the new technology, we find the fears and anxieties—the future shock, technological stress, and computer phobia—of those who must come to terms with the new tools. Already, in many offices a social distance has opened between computer users and non-users. Our fears and anxieties reflect a deeper cultural confusion about the meaning of the new technology. Does it benefit us or is it threatening? In using computers, our actions and, in turn, our thoughts are subtly changed. Our conceptions of ourselves and of machines are altered. Do we think like computers? Are computers thinking machines? A new cultural synthesis will eventually emerge in the answers to these questions. In the meantime, many will experience anxiety and uncertainty about computers.

The Global Network and the Ethos of the Information Society

From one perspective, the emerging information society results from the operation of technological imperatives. But we must also consider the aspirations of those who have championed the computer. Among computer scientists and engineers there is a shared vision of an intelligent world built around a human-computer symbiosis. In this vision, a monitored environment emerges from the deployment of dedicated microprocessors, computers, and networks overseen by programmers, intelligent programs, and scientists. The global network becomes the basis of a planetary nervous system, allowing planning, prediction, feedback, and control on a broad scale. The weather satellites that provide data for weather prediction and agricultural planning are examples of the movement toward an intelligently perceived and controlled environment. On a much smaller scale, the control of building and home environments using sensors and microprocessors linked to computers illustrates the same advance.

An outstanding example of the growth of global information resources can be seen in the ongoing NASA development of data systems for multidisciplinary research. As an adjunct of the U.S. space program, earth-sensing satellite systems have provided a profusion of planetary data for analysis and research. NASA has recently created an online system to make these multisensor data sets available for scientific study. At this stage, four pilot data systems have been inaugurated—the Pilot Climate Data System (1979), the Pilot Ocean Data System (1980), the Pilot Planetary Data System (1982), and the Pilot Land Data System (1985).

Each of the pilot data systems comprises a network linking NASA data archives with a number of user sites (universities and research centers). The systems allow researchers remote access to data directories, catalogs, and data sets for analysis. By exploring different avenues of data management and processing, the pilot systems are providing models for a larger Earth Observing Information System that NASA intends to develop for the research community. This larger system will handle the increasing multiple-sensor data inputs from future satellites and the projected space station of the 1990s. The Earth Observing System will be part of a more general Science and Applications Information System designed for mission planning, payload command and control, as well as data delivery and processing.

Although the NASA information systems for earth observation will grow in complexity, the problem of creating a global-sensing and data bank system with remote access for the scientific community is no longer a matter of science fantasy. Similar problems of global sensing and data management are involved in U.S. Defense Department strategic planning and in the proposed design of the Strategic Defense Initiative (SDI, or Star Wars). The military has established a satellite network, the Global Positioning System, for precise navigation coordinates and land position. Accurate coordinates are required to position planes, ships, missiles, and targets in the battlefield extending beyond the horizon anticipated by military planners. Another group of satellites, operated by the intelligence agencies, provides highly detailed surveillance photographs. Given the existing satellite systems for global observation, the development of a global environment information and monitoring system is technically within reach.

The information systems that augment our knowledge of the environment are also augmenting our knowledge of human institutions and society. The design and use of a global social information system is technically feasible. The number of social information data banks is growing at a rapid rate. In government, university, and business spheres,computer networks link experts and professionals with scientific and proprietary business databases. But major obstacles exist in locating and communicating information within and between these networks, let alone in extending the networks to the broader reaches of society. The difference between the type of information available to specialists through computer data banks and the information conveyed to the layman through the mass news media will not readily disappear. The increasing production and specialization of scientific and technical knowledge works against detailed communication to the public.

In governmental decision making, the use of scientific information and analysis often runs counter to purely political considerations. Nevertheless, expert testimony to government commissions shows an increasing reliance on scientific information and modelling of alternatives. In this way, government decisions are increasingly drawn into the what-if world of computer simulation. The reliance on computer data in the political process is reinforced by the mass media, which require a daily supply of new facts and work to continually extend the range and quantity of news conveyed to the public. The disaster at the Chernobyl nuclear power station in 1986 illustrated the global need for accurate information to respond to the disaster as well as the obstacles that existing social systems and political hostilities place in the way of obtaining such information. The widely felt sense of dismay at the failure of the Soviet government to inform their own population and other societies of the potential radiation hazards is a clear measure of the emerging values and norms of the information society. Irrespective of the political system, the new information systems, built on cybernetic principles of monitoring, feedback, and control, require accountablility at all institutional levels if they are to work properly. The Soviet failure to inform its population, its allies, and the world at large violated these principles. The new Soviet policy of *glasnost,* whatever its political rationale, mandates in the Soviet system the accurate accountability that is critical for the operation of an advanced society. In Western societies, the impacts of oil spills and other environmental disasters have had similar political repercussions.

As the global communications network is extended, increasing pressure is placed on all societies to conform to the ethos and norms of the information society. The focus of attention in the mass media shifts easily from society to society, highlighting instances of deviation from the emergent norms of openness and accountability. Political leaders, irrespective of ideology, are forced to respond to the media and to yield to the pressure for accurate information. Although political and cultural differences between societies remain, the norms of the information society develop along with the use of computers, communications, and information systems.

Information Society 2000

At the suburban fringe of existing cities, the main sites of microprocessor and computer manufacture, a new pattern of social life is emerging. From Silicon Valley in California to Route 128 near Boston to Britain's M4 corridor, high-technology companies and jobs have flourished. Beginning with groups of university-trained engineers and scientists, a distinctive world of new companies, technological innovation, and a fast-paced lifestyle has been created. The high-technology suburb is seen as a model of future trends in the post-industrial society. In the United States and abroad, cities and states try to emulate the success of such areas by creating high-technology parks in suburban open spaces or urban renewal areas to attract new companies.

Alongside the lifestyle of high-technology areas, new channels of communication and computer applications are changing the worlds of work and leisure. The first four decades of computerization have given us the computer conference, electronic mail, telecommuting, telework, office automation, computer-aided design, videotext, and computer banking. Further changes will come with local-area networks, factory automation, robots, artificial intelligence, and smart cards.

Beyond changes in work and leisure, electronic information is more available throughout the society. In many cases, although they are part of our everyday activities, we do not notice the presence of microprocessors. Information is captured, relayed to computers, and stored for later use with little intrusion in the flow of daily life. Financial transactions entered at the point of sale or at an electronic teller are examples of the increasing real-time capture of information. Computer users call up information from widely dispersed databases and analyse the information for a particular purpose. In the near future, artificial intelligence programs designed to consider various alternatives and explain their reasoning process will help us with decisions. In model automated factories, the interaction of machines, microprocessors, computer programs, and databases goes on largely without human intervention. Only breakdowns, changes in programs, or maintenance require human technicians to take an active role.

The computers and communications network increasingly constitutes an information structure parallel to and congruent with the world of human activities. Although computer-controlled automation is planned for the industrial factory, computer coordination of office and household machines is also feasible. Through computer coordination of the financial and technological worlds, the vast minutiae of human activities enter the computer data bank. The transparent capture of information, already present with credit card use, will become commonplace for other transactions and activities. The parallel world of information, stored in large data banks and single memory chips, will be both invisible and all-encompassing.

Notes

1. Ithiel de Sola Pool, *Forecasting the Telephone: A Retrospective Technology Assessment* (Norwood, New Jersey: Ablex Publishing, 1983), p. 13.

2. *Ibid.,* p. 7.

3. Marshall McLuhan, *Understanding Media* (New York: McGraw-Hill, 1964), p. 271.

Selected Bibliography

Barquin, Ramon, and Graham Mead, eds. *Towards the Information Society* (Amsterdam: North-Holland, 1984).

Bell, Daniel. *The Coming of Post-Industrial Society* (New York: Basic Books, 1973).

Bjorn-Andersen, Niels, M. Earl, O. Holst, and E. Mumford, eds. *Information Society* (Amsterdam: North-Holland, 1982).

de Sola Pool, Ithiel. *Forecasting the Telephone: A Retrospective Technology Assessment* (Norwood, New Jersey: Ablex Publishing, 1983).

Dutton, William, Jay Blumler, and Kenneth Kraemer, eds. *Wired Cities* (Boston, Massachusetts: G. K. Hall, 1987).

Ellul, Jacques. *The Technological Society* (New York: Random House, 1964).

Hall, Peter, and Ann Markusen, eds. *Silicon Landscapes* (Boston, Massachusetts: Allen and Unwin, 1985).

Hiltz, Starr Roxanne. *Online Communities* (Norwood, New Jersey: Ablex Publishing, 1984).

Kobayashi, Koji. *Computers and Communications* (Cambridge, Massachusetts: MIT Press, 1986).

McLuhan, Marshall. *Understanding Media* (New York: McGraw-Hill, 1964).

Marples, David. *The Social Impact of the Chernobyl Disaster* (New York: St. Martin's Press, 1988).

Martin, James. *The Wired Society* (Englewood Cliffs, New Jersey: Prentice Hall, 1978).

Masuda, Yoneji. *The Information Society* (Tokyo: Institute for the Information Society, 1980).

Naisbitt, John. *Megatrends* (New York: Warner Books, 1984).

Nora, Simon, and Alain Minc. *The Computerization of Society* (Cambridge, Massachusetts: The MIT Press, 1980).

Rogers, Everett, and Judith Larsen. *Silicon Valley Fever* (New York: Basic Books, 1984).

Schement, Jorge, and Leah Lievrouw. *Competing Visions, Complex Realities: Social Aspects of the Information Society* (Norwood, New Jersey: Ablex Publishing, 1987).

Toffler, Alvin. *The Third Wave* (New York: Bantam Books, 1981).

Winner, Langdon. *Autonomous Technology* (Cambridge, Massachusetts: The MIT Press, 1977).

A Brief History
of Computers

The creation of the computer was in one sense the culmination of several centuries of technological innovation and in another sense the outcome of the technical necessities of World War II. The prehistory of the modern computer stretches back to the various devices and tables that have been invented to aid calculation and measurement, from the abacus, astrolabe, and sextant to Napier's multiplication rods, logarithms, and the slide rule. These devices were applied in the keeping of accounts, navigation, surveying, gunnery, and engineering. The abacus, Napier's rods, and the slide rule provided means for the manual manipulation of large numbers but lacked the automatic and programmable characteristics we associate with the computer.

In the seventeenth century, several mathematicians and inventors recognized that clockwork technology could be applied to the problem of calculation just as it had been applied to the accurate measurement of time. Mechanical calculator models were created independently by Wilhelm Schickard (1592–1635), Blaise Pascal (1623–1662), Gottfried Wilhelm Leibnitz (1646–1716), and Samuel Morland (1625–1695). Only Pascal's machine, of which about fifty were made, was well known in its time. Practical mechanical calculating machines were not produced in commercial quantities until the late nineteenth century, when the practices of accounting and business enterprise created sufficient demand for them. Burroughs introduced the first commercially successful U.S. adding machine, an arithmometer, in 1891. In 1915, the largest capacity adding machine in the world had forty rows of keys and would add to within a unit of ten duodecillions. Electric adding machines introduced in the 1930s were the main type of office calculator into the 1960s. The major adding machine and office equipment manufacturers—Burroughs, IBM, Remington, and NCR—later became the first manufacturers of commercial computers.

Charles Babbage and Computing Engines

In the early nineteenth century, the English inventor and scientist Charles Babbage (1791–1871) designed a mechanical computer, the difference engine, combining the elements of computation, logic, and programmability with mechanisms for number input and output. Babbage was interested in the problem of producing accurate mathematical tables for use in navigation. He constructed a model of the computer that could be programmed to use the method of constant differences to rapidly solve polynomials. In 1822, Babbage applied to the British government for financial support in constructing a full-scale engine. The government needed the mathematical tables for the navy and approved the request in 1823.

Babbage began to build the difference engine, but in moving from model to full-scale machine he discovered that the toolmaking techniques of the time could not produce parts to the tolerances required. This made it necessary for Babbage, in conjunction with the skilled toolmakers he hired, to invent new techniques to produce parts for the engine. Babbage covered the costs of invention and design from his own income and then sought reimbursement from the British government. The project was delayed by lack of funds and changes in design; after a decade of work, the difference engine remained incomplete.

From Babbage's plans, we know that the difference engine "would have been about 10 ft. high, 10 ft. wide, and 5 ft. deep. It was to be composed of seven vertical steel axles, each of which would carry 18 brass wheels about 5 in. in diameter. Each vertical axle would represent one of the six orders or differences while the seventh axle would store the value of the function being computed. These values were represented on the axles by the positions of the 18 brass wheels."[1] When performing computations, the engine

was to operate in four distinct cycles, each one corresponding to a quarter turn of the drive wheel. The first cycle caused the numbers represented by the first, third, and fifth difference axles to be added to the numbers stored on the result, second, and fourth difference axles, respectively. The second cycle took care of any carries which may have resulted from the first cycle. The third cycle caused the addition of the second, fourth, and sixth differences to the first, third, and fifth while the last cycle again took care of any carries generated.[2]

The output mechanism of the engine would impress the results of the calculations into a soft metal plate from which a printing plate could be cast. In this way, any error in the tables that could result from typesetting would be eliminated.

By 1833, Babbage recognized the computational limitations of the difference engine and began work on a more powerful mechanism for computation, the analytical engine, to solve more complex equations. As described by Lady Ada Lovelace, the analytical engine would have used punched cards for data entry and would have been programmed for automatic operation. In their discussions, Lady Lovelace and Babbage anticipated many programming techniques including retrieval of values from memory and conditional if-then program branching. Lady Lovelace is today honored as the first programmer, and the programming language ADA bears her name. The computer designs and ideas developed by Babbage and Ada Lovelace anticipated many of the functions of memory, process, and program found in the modern computer.

Whatever the theoretical advances embodied in the design of the analytical engine, the British government refused to invest more money in Babbage's inventions and the analytical engine was never constructed. After Babbage's death, his son, Henry P. Babbage, constructed a working model of the computational mill that was at the core of the analytical engine. In Sweden, George Scheutz and his son Edvard, inspired by a newspaper account of Babbage's effort, successfully built a difference engine. The Scheutzes completed a working model of the engine in 1843, and in 1851 received a grant from the Swedish government for a full-scale machine, which they completed in 1853. In operation, "the Scheutz machine could generate 120 lines of a table per hour. In one experiment it generated logarithms of the numbers from 1 to 10,000 in just under 80 hours, including the time taken to reset the differences for the 20 different approximating polynomials used."[3] Despite the success of the Scheutz difference engine, only two were built. The first was purchased by the Dudley Observatory in Albany, New York; the second was built for the British Register General to produce tables of vital statistics.

The work of Babbage and the Scheutzes directly anticipated the widespread commercial use of mechanical calculators at the end of the nineteenth century. However, the further evolution of a general purpose computer required the combination of practical means for programmed control, memory, computation, and power that were not fully available until the twentieth century. One important element, the punched card designed for data storage and machine control, was developed early in the nineteenth century. In 1801, Joseph Jacquard (1752–1834) created a mechanism that used punched cards to control the pattern woven in cloth by a mechanical loom, the first use of punched cards to store a program and control a machine function. Jacquard's loom was commercially successful, and within a decade more than 10,000 were in use in France. Babbage was aware of the Jacquard loom, and planned to use punched cards for programming the analytical engine and for data input.

The use of punched cards to store numerical data was pioneered by Herman Hollerith (1860–1929). Hollerith had won the contract to record and then tabulate the 1890 census of the United States. He designed all aspects of the coding and tabulating process, including the fields on the cards and the electromechanical machines for tabulation. As a result of these innovations, the census was tabulated in two years, a marked improvement over the seven years taken to manually tabulate the previous census. Following his success with the census, Hollerith formed the Tabulating Machine Company to provide for commercial applications of his inventions. The company became the International Business Machines Corporation in 1924.

In the 1920s and 1930s, university scientists and engineers created the technical and theoretical basis for the general purpose, electronic digital computer. Between 1927 and 1930, Dr. Vannevar Bush at MIT built an electromechanical analog computer, the differential analyzer, to solve single-variable differential equations. The analyzer required a careful mechanical setting of gears, discs, and shafts before a problem could be run. This lengthy setup limited the practicality of analog machines and mechanical slippage limited the accuracy of the computations. Nevertheless, differential analyzers were used extensively through the 1930s and 1940s to solve equations, and the analyzer design influenced the design of the first electronic computers.

The transition from analog to digital computation needed a theoretical foundation. In the nineteenth century, the mathematician George Boole had developed a system of symbolic logic, Boolean algebra, that represented logical operations as a sequence of equations that could be verified. In 1937, Claude Shannon, a student of Dr. Bush, wrote his doctoral thesis, "A Symbolic Analysis of Relay and Switching Circuits." The thesis demonstrated that the open or closed state of electric switching circuits could represent Boolean logic in a binary form. Shannon's work provided the theoretical basis for the use of electromechanical switching circuits and, later, vacuum tubes to represent formal mathematics and logic, thereby opening the path to digital computation and electronic computers.

In 1936, the British mathematician Alan Turing provided another part of the theoretical foundation for digital logic and computation in a paper that described an abstract model of a computer. The model, which has come to be known as a Turing machine, consists of a box through which a tape of indeterminant length runs. Like motion picture film, the tape is divided into squares. A window in the box allows viewing of one square at a time. A number, a mathematical or logical operation, or some other symbol can appear in a square. In carrying out a computation, the tape can be moved one square at a time in either direction and symbols can be added, altered, or deleted. In his paper, Turing demonstrated that such a linear mechanism could be used to solve any finite computational problem no matter how complex. Turing worked on the development of code-breaking machines in England during World War II, and his ideas influenced the design of the first British computers after the war.

In the United States, George Stibitz developed an electromechanical relay computer at Bell Laboratories in 1937. A larger general purpose relay computer, an automatic sequence controlled calculator called the Mark I, was built at Harvard during the war by a team lead by Howard Aiken, in collaboration with IBM engineers. The project, funded by the U.S. Navy, was completed in 1944. The sequence of operations in the Mark I was controlled by a strip of punched paper tape. Data were read from other strips of paper tape, and computation was performed on ten position wheels:

> A mechanical desk calculator indicates numbers by digits printed on the wheels themselves, but that was not the case with the Mark I. It stored and counted numbers mechanically, but it transmitted and read those numbers electrically. A wiper attached to each wheel made contact with one of ten wires, one for each decimal digit, and that indicated the wheel's position. And the wheels were turned not by a mechanical linkage but by an electric motor that advanced the wheel to a position that corresponded to the number it was supposed to represent.[4]

The Mark I was used for the computation of tables of mathematical functions, the same purpose that had inspired Babbage's work a century earlier.

The First Electronic Computers

The substitution of vacuum tubes for electromechanical relays set the stage for the electronic digital computer. A model electronic digital computer was built by John Atanasoff and his assistant, Clifford Berry, at Iowa State University between 1939 and 1942. The computer combined a vacuum-tube computation unit with a rotating electrostatic memory drum. For reasons of simplicity, Atanasoff chose binary over decimal arithmetic for computation. Although Atanasoff and Berry completed the computer, war research assignments took them away from Iowa State in 1942 and they did not pursue further development of their computer. Atanasoff's machine languished in a basement, but his ideas influenced John Mauchly and, through him, the design of ENIAC. Mauchly had corresponded with Atanasoff in 1940 and visited him in Iowa in 1941. Atanasoff demonstrated his computer to Mauchly during the visit. Mauchly later denied that his computer designs were influenced by Atanasoff, but a court case in 1971 found otherwise.[5]

The first general purpose electronic computer, ENIAC (electronic numerical integrator and calculator), was designed by J. Presper Eckert and John Mauchly at the Moore School of Electrical Engineering under a contract with the U.S. Army. The machine was intended to speed the preparation of firing tables required for artillery during World War II but was not operational until 1945. ENIAC used punched cards for input, operated with 18,000 vacuum tubes, and had a speed of 100,000 pulses per second. This was 500 times faster than electromechanical relay computers. ENIAC was modeled in part on the differential analyzer, and the units of the computer operated in parallel. Each unit was set or programmed manually on its front panel and connected by patch wires to the other units. After data were entered from the cards, computation was automatic until the results were obtained. To change the program, the computer units had to be manually reset.

The second electronic computer Eckert and Mauchly developed at the Moore School, EDVAC (electronic discrete variable computer), was very different from ENIAC. It incorporated an internally stored program for control, a single instruction stream for the central processor, and binary arithmetic for computations. These changes were in part the contribution of mathematician John von Neumann, who worked with Eckert and Mauchly. Von Neumann described the features of the EDVAC design in a paper, "First Draft of a Report on the EDVAC," written in 1945 and widely circulated in typescript. Von Neumann's writings on the EDVAC and on a subsequent computer he collaborated on at the Institute for Advanced Study at Princeton became the basis for von Neumann architecture, the sequential, single-stream processing structure of most modern computers. After EDVAC, Eckert and Mauchly left the Moore School and set up a company to produce the first commercial electronic computer—UNIVAC (universal automatic computer).

Computer Generations

From the first generation of vacuum tube computers, computer design advanced through developments in hardware and software. On the hardware side, the computer changed with the replacement of vacuum tubes by transistors, the progressive miniaturization of integrated circuitry, and the development of enhanced electronic memory. The transistor, which John Bardeen, Walter Brattain, and William Shockley invented at Bell Laboratories in 1948, did not completely replace the vacuum tube in computers until the beginning of the 1960s. The second generation of computers was based on transistors and magnetic core memory. Although Robert Noyce at Fairchild Semiconductor and Jack Kilby at Texas Instruments independently invented the integrated circuit in the late 1950s, it was too expensive and untested for widespread commercial use. Military applications of integrated circuits in the rocket and space flight programs, where weight and size were of great importance, proved the reliablity of integrated circuit technology.

The third generation of computers, based on integrated circuits and semiconductor memory, appeared in the late 1960s. From the 1970s on, rapid advances in large-scale integration of transistors on silicon chips, inexpensive random access memory, and microprocessors led to the production of powerful fourth-generation mainframes, midsize minicomputers, personal computers, and workstations. Throughout this period, the steady advance of semiconductor technology allowed the number of transistors on a chip to double year by year, reaching current levels of 500,000 transistors integrated on a square centimeter. Chips with one million elements are now in production.

On the software side, the development of operating systems, computer languages, programming techniques, and applications accompanied the changes in hardware. The first computers were programmed with assembly language code. As this method was difficult and time consuming, programming languages evolved quickly through second-generation intermediate code to third-generation high-level languages. In 1953, John Backus at IBM developed the first high-level language, FORTRAN, for scientific applications. In 1959, Grace Hopper directed the creation of COBOL, a language for commercial and record-keeping applications. The movement from batch processing to time-sharing systems with terminals in the 1960s and 1970s led to the development of more interactive languages such as BASIC and APL. Programmers have also written many special purpose languages for artificial intelligence (LISP and PROLOG), simulation (GPSS, SNOBOL, and SIMULA), and other uses.

In recent years, as computer scientists became concerned with program clarity and efficiency they created structured modular languages such as Pascal and Modula 2. Structured modular programs are more easily understood and maintained than was previously the case. Some fourth-generation languages and software have moved from a procedure-oriented to an object-oriented approach for the control of information in the computer. Such fourth-generation software allows the user to create (program) applications by visual programming or making selections from a menu. However, most large programs continue to be written by programmers in procedure-oriented languages.

As computer languages have evolved from first to fourth generation, the user has been moved farther and farther from the hardware of the machine. Recent software and languages have tended toward an almost natural language or icon interface. The end user is insulated from the rigors of third-generation programming. A third-generation programming potential may be embedded in a fourth-generation application, but the users do not usually need to do any programming. They can begin productive use of an application in a matter of hours. When fifth-generation intelligent assistant programs are integrated into the existing fourth-generation software, there will be even less call for the user to program the machine.

Project Whirlwind, SAGE, and IBM System/360

In the early years of mainframe development, government funding of computers for military purposes was critically important. The cold war fears of the 1950s and the need for an extensive system of radar protection for the United States led to the creation of the first online realtime network—SAGE (semi-automatic ground environment). In 1948, Project Whirlwind at MIT began the first steps toward a computer capable of realtime applications, with funding from the office of naval research. Engineers under the direction of Jay Forrester designed the Whirlwind computer for speed and reliability. It used 4,000 tubes, compared with ENIAC's 18,000, and shorter sixteen-bit words. Internal memory initially used electrostatic tubes that required frequent replacement. To improve the memory, Forrester invented the magnetic core storage system in 1949, but it was not fully operational until 1953.

In 1950, the military and the engineers began to alter the Whirlwind computer for the SAGE radar defense system. This required linking the computer to a radar system to track airplanes and designing software for realtime tracking and course determination. They tested the design successfully in 1951, and a complete system of twenty-three defense centers was planned, each with its own computer. The contract for these improved versions of the Whirlwind computer went to IBM. The first SAGE center went into operation in 1958. The SAGE computers, containing 55,000 vacuum tubes, were the largest of the first-generation computers. But more importantly, the SAGE system served as a working model for a computer and terminals network. For example, the realtime seat reservation system that IBM designed for American Airlines followed the pattern set by the SAGE system.

In the 1950s, competing computer companies produced several types of vacuum-tube machines for scientific, military, and commercial applications. These machines changed rapidly during the decade as different modes of internal memory and magnetic storage were used. The IBM 705, introduced in 1956, featured a 40,000-character memory that increased to 60,000 characters in 1957 and 80,000 characters in 1959. For mass data storage, IBM developed plastic tape drives that replaced the metal-backed tapes used on the first UNIVACs. However, the different types of machines produced by a single manufacturer were often not compatible, and the machines of different companies were also incompatible. Computer users could not migrate from small machines to larger ones without a significant disruption in their data processing system.

For the 1960s, IBM decided to create a new line of compatible computers. Integrated circuit technology was still experimental, so the machines were designed around small ceramic modules composed of individual transistors (in later years, these modules were replaced by integrated circuits). The new line, System/360, was announced in 1964 and set the pattern for compatible families produced by other manufacturers. The success of System/360 made IBM the dominant company in the computer marketplace. New companies emerged to produce plug-compatible peripheral equipment for System/360 computers. A similar pattern developed in the 1980s after the success of the IBM Personal Computer.

Computer-Serviced Subcultures

As mainframe computing developed in the 1960s, there was a gradual transition from batch processing with its long turnaround times to interactive time-sharing networks. This change was viewed as a step forward in terms of machine accessibility and rapid program debugging. Harold Sackman, in his 1967 book *Computers, System Science, and Evolving Society,* gave a detailed account of the evolution and characteristics of online networks.[6] To describe the institutional role of online networks, Sackman developed the concept of a computer-serviced subculture using the evolution of the SAGE system as an example:

> SAGE is a geographically dispersed, multi-computer system with lateral communication between adjacent Direction Centers and vertical communication upward to Combat Centers and downward to BUIC [backup interceptor control] sites. This distributed and computerized network, involving thousands of personnel with a formal division of labor, embedded in an established military structure (NORAD) in the United States and Canada, is the first of the computer-serviced subcultures. Experience with SAGE is useful for examining and anticipating emergent problems of other computer-serviced subcultures, which are beginning to arise in large-scale civilian applications.[7]

In the SAGE system, human decision making is uppermost. The computer system supports and implements the air defense decisions made by military personnel. The computer-serviced subculture is integrated with the hierarchy of military authority. The computer network designed for the Mercury manned spaceflight project followed the SAGE pattern. The design of the SAGE and Mercury projects allows system testing in realtime, monitoring and analysis of ongoing events, and playback of events from the computer memory.

In a following work, *Mass Information Utilities and Social Excellence,* Sackman extended his analysis of computer-serviced subcultures by proposing the establishment of computer utilities.[8] For industries such as the natural gas distribution network and the telephone network that tended toward a natural monopoly, the government has authorized the establishment of public utility companies. Regulated by public utility commissions, these industries are required to provide service to all customers at a reasonable price. By analogy, Sackman argued that large computer networks were a social resource and should be developed in the public interest. By providing many computer services to subscribers at reasonable costs, the computer utility would speed the flow of information and serve as a framework for social improvement in government, education, and business. The government has not created regulated computer utilities, but The Source, CompuServe, and other large database vendors are close in function to what Sackman proposed.

In his study of time-sharing networks, Sackman found a link betweeen the stages of system implementation and end-user activities. In the network design and installation phases, users explored the system, expressing frustrations and complaints. As the system evolved toward an operating steady state, users became more familiar with the network and were concerned with system applications and customization to meet their personal needs. On a network in use at the Massachusetts Institute of Technology (MIT):

> The users have "taken over" in the sense that they are the focus of system direction and change—most of the object programs were written by users rather than system programmers. The users organized their own editorial and referee boards to decide on new commands and revised conventions, and to decide which information should be stored in public files. Joint problem-solving was starting to take place between users at different remote stations working with the same problem and data base, as it did with students and teachers and with members of the same research team.[9]

Sackman suggested that cooperative problem solving by users would become a common activity on networks. While the MIT network users were not typical end users, Sackman's study revealed the importance of the nascent user community on a network system.

However, until recently, the evolution of computer time-sharing networks has not usually emphasized the user community or cooperative problem solving. Outside of universities and information networks such as The Source or CompuServe, the institutional network user at a terminal has been allowed only restricted use of the system. In the military, government, and financial networks, only authorized groups of system specialists are allowed access to the entire system. These institutions emphasize system and data security over the formation of a user community. As users begin to share resources on local-area networks, group work and cooperative problem solving are becoming part of the institutional computer culture.

To the general public, institutional computer-serviced subcultures at times convey a feeling of computer tyranny. Because such systems place the user in a passive position, they arouse a desire to subvert or crack the system. Institutional computers have reinforced hierarchical power arrangements by controlling the flow of information and limiting unauthorized access. This situation has been broadly dramatized in several movies, most notably *War Games*. In the movie, a hacker who's broken into the air force network plays a realtime air defense game with the network mainframe. The game is taken by the system's military operators to be a real missile and bomber attack. As the game escalates from one level of alert to another, the military operators find themselves unable to arrest the nuclear missile launch sequence.

The movie ends happily when the computer comes to its senses. In actuality, however, the computer might not have that degree of autonomy. For example, in the movies *Colossus: The Forbin Project* and *2001: A*

Space Odyssey, the mainframe computers are more negatively portrayed as giant brains that run amok and destroy people to complete the assigned mission. The popular success of *War Games* suggests a public awareness of the dilemmas of computer-serviced societies. Once the game begins, the military operators are powerless and the computerized system is out of control. Only the hacker and the disillusioned scientist, both rulebreakers, are able to act. *War Games* recognizes that people will play games with computers even though we know we aren't supposed to. The computer is portrayed ambivalently as both an instrument of destruction and an instrument of hope, which may be a realistic assessment.

Minicomputers and the Personal Computer

The expectations about computer-serviced subcultures and computer utilities in the 1960s reflected the world of time-sharing networks and mainframe computers. As integrated circuit technology advanced, however, new types of computers were designed that drastically altered the size, cost, and uses of the machines. The first minicomputer based on transistor technology, the PDP-8, was introduced by Digital Equipment Corporation in 1963. A small machine with limited memory (4K) and limited processing power, the PDP-8 was designed for use by small companies and laboratories that could not afford a mainframe but wished to be independent of time-sharing facilities. The market for minicomputers expanded rapidly as many uses were found for these cabinet-size machines.

The development of large-scale integrated circuits in the 1970s made possible a further reduction in the size of both mainframes and minicomputers, while computing power and memory were increased. Through the decade and into the 1980s, the speed and memory of computers doubled each year while cost fell. Whether through mainframe purchase, data processing services, time sharing, or minicomputers, more and more institutional tasks were shifted to computers. The possibility of designing a computer for unrestricted personal use became feasible after 1971, when Intel produced the first microprocessors, or computers on chips. The first hobbyist computer kits appeared in 1975, and a score of personal computer companies quickly followed.

The hobbyist microcomputers built in the late 1970s had limited memory (16 to 64 kilobytes) and software. The situation changed rapidly as a number of start-up companies pioneered various standards: the S-100 bus, the CPM operating system, the BASIC programming language, and WordStar and Visicalc applications software. By the early 1980s, when IBM entered the market, the microcomputer had begun to have standardized appearance, floppy disk drives, line-driven operating system, and applications. The market quickly followed the path taken by IBM, and the IBM-type personal computer and operating system (MS-DOS) became the industry standards. With the exception of Apple computers, users required IBM PC–compatible machines that would run PC software. Most personal computer companies competed by producing clones of the IBM standard machine or additional equipment such as add-in boards and hard disk drives. Software companies also developed their products for IBM-compatible machines or for Apple computers.

The hobbyist microcomputers were not the first desktop computers. While the predominant mainframe computing model was maturing in the 1970s, an alternative model based on the desktop computer was developed at the Xerox Palo Alto Research Center (PARC). Researchers at PARC designed and built an innovative computer, the Alto, that combined an icon-based interface, a mouse, and object-oriented programming. The desktop machines were linked in a local-area network (Ethernet). The Alto was a decade ahead of the machines built by hobbyists, but Xerox did not bring a commercial version, the Star, to market until 1982. By that time, the course of microcomputer development had been set by MITS, Cromenco, IMSAI, Morrow, Apple, Osborne, and IBM. As alternatives to the IBM standard machine, the Apple LISA and Macintosh computers used an icon-based interface, a bit-mapped screen, and a mouse derived in part from the research at Xerox PARC.

Since 1985, microcomputers have become faster and incorporated increasingly more memory (640K to 2 megabytes and beyond), gaining the ability to handle more applications. In 1989, Everex Systems, a personal computer manufacturer, compiled processor speed benchmarks for some of the machines using Intel 80286 and 80386 microprocessors (see Table 2.1). These machines achieve processing speeds previously found only in larger computers. Although IBM-compatible machines continue to dominate the personal computer marketplace, IBM itself is moving to a new line of machines (PS/2) with a different internal bus (Micro Channel) and a new operating system (OS/2). At the same time, Apple has been able to expand the speed and memory of the Macintosh computers, which have been successful alternatives to the IBM standard PC because of their ease of use, application software, and graphics capabilities.

The current generation of Intel 80386 and Motorola 68030 microprocessors used in advanced personal computers and workstations are like mainframe processors in their support of 32-bit architecture, virtual memory, and multitasking. The fastest personal computers are designed with an instruction cache memory to allow the processor to operate at high speeds. As personal computers increase in speed and

Table 2.1
Personal Computer Processing Speeds

Computer/MHz	MIPS (million instructions per second)
Everex Step 386/33	8.3
Everex Step 386/25	6.1
Compaq Deskpro 386/25	5.5
Everex Step 386/20	4.91
Compaq Deskpro 386/20	4.59
Everex Step 386/16	3.93
AST Premium 386/20	3.04
Wyse 386/16	2.98
Compaq Deskpro 386/16	2.90
IBM PS/2 Model 80, 386/16	2.87
Everex Step 286/12	2.45
AST Premium 286/10	2.02
Compaq Deskpro 286/12	1.89
IBM PS/2 Models 50 and 60	1.56
IBM PC AT 286/8	0.93

Source: Everex Systems, 1989.

memory, they are approaching the power of specialized engineering workstations. In workstations, a new type of microprocessor designed with a reduced instruction set architecture (RISC—reduced instruction set computer) is being used to produce desktop machines with processing speeds from 10 million to 20 million instructions per second (MIPS). In graphics workstations such as those designed by Silicon Graphics, custom graphics chips work with the microprocessor to allow rapid three-dimensional modeling. In another special application, Texas Instruments has designed an artificial intelligence workstation by placing a custom LISP language chip in a Macintosh II computer. Although the general purpose personal computer is converging in power with the engineering workstation, we can also anticipate more custom chip workstation designs for special applications.

The faster personal computers and graphics workstations can match the power of minicomputers and some mainframes. As computing power moves to the desktop this will, in time, change the computer marketplace and the way computers are used. Companies in the United States, Asia, and Europe that manufacture computers, semiconductors, and communications equipment are engaged in an extremely competitive arena. According to *Datamation* magazine, the top 100 information technology companies sold $243.1 billion of products and services in 1988.[10] The fifteen leading information technology companies worldwide are listed in Table 2.2. As new hardware and software are developed,

Table 2.2
Leading Worldwide Information Technology Companies

Company	1988 Information systems revenue (millions of dollars)
1. IBM	55,002.8
2. Digital Equipment	12,284.7
3. Fujitsu	10,999.1
4. NEC	10,475.7
5. Unisys	9,100.0
6. Hitachi	8,247.6
7. Hewlett-Packard	6,300.0
8. Siemens	5,951.0
9. Olivetti	5,427.9
10. NCR	5,324.0
11. Groupe Bull	5,296.7
12. Apple	4,434.1
13. Toshiba	4,226.6
14. Matsushita	3,441.0
15. Canon	3,391.6

Source: Joseph Kelly, "Three Markets Shape Our Society," *Datamation,* Vol. 35, No. 12, June 15, 1989, p. 11. Reprinted with permission.

the competitive advantage of companies can shift dramatically. U.S. companies enjoyed an early advantage in semiconductors and the computer arena, but Japanese and European companies are now challenging U.S. dominance. Success in computer electronics is seen as an indicator of general future economic success, and the lead taken by Japanese companies in semiconductor memory chips and consumer electronics has been met with many dire predictions for the U.S. economy. Whatever the outcome of competition for market share in electronics, the enthusiasm and innovation surrounding the first microprocessors and personal computers has been replaced by the rapid and steady technical evolution of machines and applications. As computer companies compete in the international market, the computer and communications infrastructure in all institutions is being put into place.

Many predictions put forward before 1975 about the ways computers would be used have had to be adjusted to take into account several noteworthy changes brought about by the personal computer:

1. The personal computer, by allowing individuals to have their own machines, removed many of the obstacles that separated users from mainframes.
2. Through ease of access and portability, the personal computer user was encouraged to try using the machine in new ways, which stimulated the development of new applications.

3. The development of a user-friendly operating environment allowed refinement of techniques for using the computer as a personal tool in word and outline processing, drawing and design, data management, and a variety of other specialized areas.

Although personal and desktop computers had been anticipated by scientists, their full impact was not foreseen. The widespread use of personal computers has triggered the growth of user groups, bulletin boards, computer magazines, computer fairs, and other elements of a flourishing personal computer culture. From a tool of only large institutions and corporations, the computer has become a tool that can be used generally in society. Users, once passive recipients of a computer service, have been actively involved with the computer and its software. These changes have altered the relationship between society and computers and given new meaning to the computer revolution.

Fourth-Generation Languages and Software

As computer languages and software have developed from the first to the fourth generation, the user has been moved farther and farther from any concern with the specific hardware of the machine. Fourth-generation software has been designed with user-friendly English-language or icon interfaces. Practical application software tailored to the needs of the user is commonplace; many packages include some mode for personal customization. An end user often can become proficient in using an application package in a matter of hours.

Software designers feel the key to unlocking the power of fourth- and fifth-generation hardware lies in the variety and practicality of fourth- and fifth-generation software. The machine-level codes and assembly language of the first and second generations of computer language were highly technical and difficult to use. The third generation of higher level languages from FORTRAN and COBOL to Pascal provided powerful and efficient procedure-oriented tools for programming mainframes and minicomputers. The third-generation languages required the expertise of professional programmers for the creation of custom applications. In third-generation database systems, a new report on a body of data required a new program from a programmer and a time lag of several weeks.

With fourth-generation languages and software, a new realm of high-level tools has been created. Many languages are part of relational database management systems and provide tools for the user to query the database and to design reports and graphic displays from a microcomputer. Fourth-generation software often works with a menu of commands, or an object-oriented interface. A user's selections or commands from the English-language menu must be translated by the fourth-generation language into the appropriate machine instructions, but the high cost in machine overhead is not visible to the user. Because complex applications are beyond the skills of most users, these continue to be written by professional programmers in the more efficient third-generation languages.

In the third-generation mainframe environments of the 1970s, user-friendly application software was almost nonexistent. The evolution of personal computer spreadsheet packages from Visicalc to Lotus 1-2-3 and Excel reflects the shift from third-generation dependency on data processing personnel to fourth-generation end-user autonomy. The business manager has been given an increasing number of ways in which data can be displayed, manipulated, and modeled, with a variety of different data views built into most programs. A similar evolution has occurred in word and outline processing and in graphic displays. The fifth-generation software environment promises to provide an even higher level of software integration as expert systems are incorporated in the existing fourth-generation software. Using windows and multitasking, the user will be able to work on several projects with the aid of expert style analysis, data analysis, and graphics packages. Although both fourth- and fifth-generation software require more computer power and memory per user, this has become of less concern with the decreasing cost of microprocessors and memory. Overall, end-user computing is driven by the user's desire for an accessible and rapidly responsive machine.

Supercomputers and the Fifth Generation

Although many minicomputers and personal computers of today have the capabilities of the mainframes of the 1970s, the demands of science, industry, and the military have led to the creation of powerful supercomputers. For numerically intensive computing (geologic exploration, wind tunnel simulations, molecular physics, and space and defense systems), computers capable of performing multiple gigaflops (billion floating point operations per second) are being produced. These computers, of which the Cray is the best known, use vector and parallel processing to achieve the necessary number-crunching power. Vector and parallel processing require unusual computer architecture and special programming. For vector processing, the computer architecture works with vector arrays rather than discrete scalar elements, and the numerically intensive portions of a program must be written to use this facility. To achieve full speed and power in processing vector arrays, the supercomputer must not be interrupted in the middle of its program, which limits the interactive use of supercomputers. Scientists and engineers have found that they can experiment with more design and research solutions in a short period of time on interactive engineering and graphics workstations.

Supercomputers built with a parallel processing architecture are designed to overcome the processing bottleneck caused by using a von Neumann–type single instruction stream. The parallel computer architecture must coordinate communication and timing across an array of coprocessors, and the programs for the machine must be structured to allow simultaneous computation of subroutines. Although massively parallel supercomputers, such as those made by Sequent and Floating Point Systems, are in principle faster and less expensive than the serial supercomputers, the unconventional programming required to utilize the parallel architecture has been an obstacle to wide use of the machines.

While research continues in the United States and Japan to create faster supercomputers, some of the techniques used in supercomputer architecture are being transferred to microprocessor design. Intel has recently produced a RISC microprocessor, the 80860, modeled on the Cray supercomputer. The design uses one million transistors to provide a 64-bit processor, data and instruction caches, integer and floating-point math units, and a graphics processor. The math units can operate in parallel using a pipelining system and the data cache. Integrating these functions on a single chip makes it possible to sustain high processor speed over time. The Intel 80860 and similar RISC chips produced by Sun, MIPS, and Motorola are intended to power interactive engineering and three-dimensional graphics workstations.

Computer designers expect that future fifth-generation computers will be based on further advances in microchip density, parallel and vector processing, and artificial intelligence techniques. The design of more intelligent computers remains a goal of the computer community. The predictions of Edward Feigenbaum and Pamela McCorduck in *The Fifth Generation* reflect this aspiration:

> The Fifth Generation will stand apart not only because of its technology, but also because it is conceptually and functionally different from the first four generations the world is familiar with. These new machines will be known as knowledge information processing systems, or KIPS.
>
> That term is extremely important. It signals the shift from mere data processing, which is the way present-day computers function, to an intelligent processing of knowledge. These new machines are to be specifically designed for artificial intelligence functions.[11]

Knowledge processing machines will incorporate and move beyond the current state of knowledge-based expert systems. Existing expert systems work with formalized knowledge in limited domains but fail with vague, ambiguous, "common sense" problems. Beyond hardware, major breakthroughs in artificial intelligence research are required before the vision of knowledge processing machines will be realized.

Whatever advances are made in computer hardware and software, computer development will continue to be influenced by the ways in which the machines are actually used. In contrast to mainframe use, which was highly centralized and restricted, the trend with personal computers and workstations is toward distributed networks, stand-alone machines, and open access. This has already led to the development of new interfaces and application software that are, in turn, changing the mainframe environment. The differences between mainframe and personal computer uses and related issues of computer accessibility will continue to mold computer development in the next decade.

Notes

1. Michael Williams, *A History of Computing Technology* (Englewood Cliffs, New Jersey: Prentice Hall, 1985), p. 172.

2. *Ibid.,* p. 173.

3. *Ibid.,* p. 178.

4. Paul Ceruzzi, *Reckoners* (Westport, Connecticut: Greenwood Press, 1983), p. 52.

5. For a detailed discussion of the work of Atanasoff and Mauchly see Alice Burks and Arthur Burks, *The First Electronic Computer* (Ann Arbor: University of Michigan Press, 1988).

6. Harold Sackman, *Computers, System Science, and Evolving Society* (New York: John Wiley and Sons, 1967).

7. *Ibid.,* p. 118.

8. Harold Sackman, *Mass Information Utilities and Social Excellence* (New York: Auerbach Publishers, 1971).

9. *Ibid.,* p. 84.

10. Joseph Kelly, "Three Markets Shape One Industry," *Datamation,* Vol. 35, No. 12, June 15, 1989, pp. 7–11.

11. Edward A. Feigenbaum and Pamela McCorduck, *The Fifth Generation* (Reading, Massachusetts: Addison-Wesley, 1983), pp. 17–18.

Selected Bibliography

Almasi, George, and Allan Gottlieb. *Highly Parallel Computing* (Redwood City, California: Benjamin/Cummings Publishing Co., 1989).

Augarten, Stan. *Bit by Bit* (New York: Ticknor and Fields, 1984).

Baron, Naomi S. *Computer Languages* (Garden City, New York: Anchor Press/ Doubleday, 1986).

Bashe, Charles, Lyle Johnson, John Palmer, and Emerson Pugh. *IBM's Early Computers* (Cambridge, Massachusetts: The MIT Press, 1986).

Braun, Ernest, and Stuart MacDonald. *Revolution in Miniature* (London: Cambridge University Press, 1978).

Burks, Alice, and Arthur Burks. *The First Electronic Computer* (Ann Arbor: University of Michigan Press, 1988).

Ceruzzi, Paul. *Reckoners* (Westport, Connecticut: Greenwood Press, 1983).

Chorafas, Dimitris N. *Fourth and Fifth Generation Programming Languages* (New York: McGraw-Hill, 1986).

Feigenbaum, Edward A., and Pamela McCorduck. *The Fifth Generation* (Reading, Massachusetts: Addison-Wesley, 1983).

Fisher, Alan. *CASE* (New York: John Wiley and Sons, 1988).

Fishman, Katharine D. *The Computer Establishment* (New York: McGraw-Hill, 1981).

Freiberger, Paul, and Michael Swaine. *Fire in the Valley* (Berkeley, California: Osborne/McGraw-Hill, 1984).

Karin, Sidney, and Norris Smith. *The Supercomputer Era* (Boston, Massachusetts: Harcourt Brace Jovanovich, 1987).

Kelly, Joseph. "Three Markets Shape One Industry." *Datamation,* Vol. 35, No. 12 (June 15, 1989): 7–11.

Lavington, Simon. *Early British Computers* (Bedford, Massachusetts: Digital Press, 1980).

Metropolis, N., D. Sharp, W. Worlton, and K. Ames. *Frontiers of Supercomputing* (Berkeley and Los Angeles: University of California Press, 1986).

Mollenhoff, Clark. *Atanasoff* (Ames: Iowa State University Press, 1988).

Pugh, Emerson. *Memories that Shaped an Industry* (Cambridge, Massachusetts: The MIT Press, 1984).

Redmond, Kent, and Thomas Smith. *Project Whirlwind* (Bedford, Massachusetts: Digital Press, 1980).

Reid, T. R. *The Chip* (New York: Simon & Schuster, 1984).

Rheingold, Howard. *Tools for Thought* (New York: Simon & Schuster, 1985).

Ritchie, David. *The Computer Pioneers* (New York: Simon & Schuster, 1986).

Sackman, Harold. *Computers, System Science, and Evolving Society* (New York: John Wiley and Sons, 1967).

Sackman, Harold. *Mass Information Utilities and Social Excellence* (New York: Auerbach Publishers, 1971).

Shurkin, Joel. *Engines of the Mind* (New York: W. W. Norton and Co., 1984).

Stern, Nancy. *From ENIAC to UNIVAC* (Bedford, Massachusetts: Digital Press, 1981).

Trask, Maurice. *The Story of Cybernetics* (New York: E. P. Dutton and Co., 1971).

Williams, Michael R. *A History of Computing Technology* (Englewood Cliffs, New Jersey: Prentice Hall, 1985).

Computer Culture

A s the industrial system evolves into an information society, our values and culture are changing. It is a common assumption of social science that the tools used by a culture reveal its distinctive strengths and weaknesses. As Lewis Mumford, Marshall McLuhan, and others have noted, all tools can be said to extend our senses and shape our perceptions. In contrast to the cognitive belief systems of earlier societies, which were composed of many transcendent myths and mysteries, the belief system of technological society has been increasingly the object and result of scientific scrutiny and review. Our material culture in this century largely consists of mass-produced products made with industrial and scientific tools. In turn, many cognitive and evaluative dimensions of our culture are determined by the values and norms of the technological and scientific worldview.

Computers and microprocessors, as elements of the material culture, belong to the special class of tools designed for information processing and storage, system control, and scientific analysis. When coupled with sensing devices, these tools enable us to extend our observation and measurement of the environment. The computer differs from other scientific tools in its general applicability, but shares with them a built-in precision and discrete logic. Of course, precision instruments or computers can be used incorrectly and can produce inaccurate results. But without such instruments, precise measurement, calculation, and analysis would be hindered. In that sense, computers are tools designed for scientific purposes in the context of a scientific culture.

In terms of our cognitive culture, the computer is used for the storage, exchange, manipulation, and analysis of information. In the past, language, writing, printing, pictures, and diagrams have all served as means for storing and exchanging information. All cultures have depended on the use of information to one degree or another, but the information itself was usually secondary to some more important cultural activity. In the computer environment, the information itself takes center stage, but this may be only partially recognized by the users. Home computer users, for example, have access via modem to many information resources but may value only information relevant to their particular interests. For the culture as a whole, the computer and associated electronic storage media mark a scalar advance in the ability to store and interpret information.

Industrial Culture

Industrial culture reflected the use of mechanized technology to change the process of production. Production work was broken into small repetitive tasks that could be organized along industrial lines. During the process of industrialization, the skilled craft worker was gradually displaced by the semiskilled or unskilled industrial worker. Industrial man, the masses of blue-collar workers, was thought of as a cog in a vast machine. Workers were expected to repeat a set of routine assembly tasks throughout the working day. This labor led to boredom, alienation, and hostility toward the industrial system.

The initial applications of science to the industrial system focused on increasing the efficiency of the system with little regard for any impact on the workers. In the first part of this century, scientific management and time and motion studies of work placed control of the manufacturing process in the hands of managers and engineers. Workers were not to have any autonomy or authority in guiding the work process and were replaced by more reliable machines where possible. This approach continues to dominate most plans for factory automation.

In material terms, industrial technology produces a wide range of standardized products from automobiles and refrigerators to toasters and lamps. The distribution of these mass-produced goods to the populace has gradually improved the standard of living in the industrial societies. Mass production and distribution of electronic goods, from telephones to radio and television, creates the framework for mass communications. Wide distribution and use of personal computers is an additional element in the communications framework. The resulting infrastructure of communications and computers provides the material basis for a widespread information-centered culture.

The Culture of Science

Popular and scientific conceptions of nature and society have changed as science and industry evolved. As we shift from the nineteenth-century mechanistic models of the world toward the predominance of electronic and computer models, our conceptions of time, space, language, memory, and thought are changing. If we define our world and ourselves in terms of computer models, we encounter a realm of finite time and space, or finite models suited to processing on a computer. A division of mental labor is developing in which certain intelligent functions are assigned to people and others are assigned to computers. Both humans and computers are viewed as examples of information processors—one slow and syncretic, the other fast and discrete. As we once recast the image of humans in mechanical terms, we now start to see that image in information system terms. Just as memorization and exact recall became less important once books were widely available, so aspects of our minds that are not needed in the information processing model may come in time to be viewed as obsolete.

The emerging information culture that is accompanying computerization is a descendant of the culture of the scientific revolution that accompanied industrialization. Since the seventeenth century, distinct scientific institutions have existed in western society. Universities, scientific societies, academies, and natural history museums fostered the discovery and use of scientific knowledge. These institutions emphasized freedom of inquiry, exchange of information, scientific specialization, and recognition of the authority of specialists. The activities of scientists and researchers have usually been self-paced and self-regulated within the collegial framework of scientific institutions.

As the culture of the information society develops, the norms of such scientific institutions are being carried along with computer systems into other institutional settings. The norms of most other institutions, from government bureaucracies to industrial corporations, tend to emphasize strict supervision of personnel and work by the clock. With computers, the new role of the knowledge worker requires both intelligence and autonomy to deal with complex systems and problems. This is very different from the restrictive role of the industrial or clerical worker, and many institutions have only begun to adjust their norms to accommodate knowledge workers.

As instruments of scientific rationality, computers and microprocessors embody a discrete and systematic information processing architecture. To be transferred to a computer, knowledge must be structured so the machine can process it. This requires the formalization of knowledge and procedures in the subject area.

For example, one would think that for a field as highly developed as medicine, clear decision-making strategies for diagnosis would have evolved by now. Yet, although clinicians make many diagnoses daily, for many diseases, few formalized decision criteria are available. From a social point of view, expert systems are likely, in the next two decades, to help systematize the more well-established reasoning procedures used by experts. They will not replace the experts, but rather help people to move into more intellectually challenging activities where the knowledge encoded in an expert system is another routine source of information.[1]

Even without expert systems, computer data storage and analysis is leading to the formalization of many areas of information. As users enter information in database systems and spreadsheets, they routinely order and rationalize the material. Increasingly, the organization of work and thought mirrors the organization of information in the computer as ways of thinking and working derived from the culture of scientific rationality move farther into the institutions of society.

The Human-Computer Interface and the Use of Information

The design and structure of the human-computer interface play an important role in determining the division of labor between humans and thinking machines. An easily understandable interface and online help make computer-based information more accessible to users. Broad participation in the information culture requires easily understandable systems.

There are several elements in the computer interface—the physical design of the machine itself, the software interface, and the cognitive structure of the information in the machine. In each of these areas different approaches are being experimented with. For the physical interface, computer manufacturers are exploring different screen sizes and placements, keyboards, the electronic mouse, and touchscreeens. Beyond keyboard input, they have designed optical character and bar code readers, scanners and digitizers, and spoken language interfaces.

Software interface options include commands, menus, icons, windows, programming and natural languages, and online help. A standard graphic icon interface, such as that on Macintosh computers, makes it possible for users to quickly understand and use all applications that share the interface. As users have shown a preference for a graphic interface, this has been adapted to more computers and become more elaborate. The NEXT workstation, for example, provides several types of windows, menus, panels, icons, buttons, scroll bars, and directories, which may be opened, resized, dragged, detached, hidden, and closed. For ease of use, there may be an upper limit to the number of options included in a graphic icon interface. Online help, usually a brief explanation of commands, has been included in many systems and software packages. Most help tutorials assume a certain familiarity with the system or application. In ideal terms, the computer interface, like the telephone keyboard, would be almost transparent to the user and require no explanation. In practical terms, interface designers try to minimize the need for online help.

As cognitive structures, information in a computer can be represented and made accessible as text, number, program, outline, hypertext, spreadsheet, record, time series, graph, map, picture, or other pattern. In fourth-generation database systems such as IDMS/R by Cullinet and INGRES by Relational Technology, the programming, data structure, query, graph, and report elements of database management are integrated into a single interface that can be accessed on mainframe or microcomputer. The INGRES user interface, for example, provides the following features:

1. The Visual Programming style of interaction is identical to other members of the INGRES family of Visual Programming tools.
2. Users specify form definitions by pointing at screen objects, filling in forms, and making menu selections.
3. Default "skeleton" forms that can be edited are constructed automatically by the Integrated Data Dictionary from table and join definitions.
4. Users define production applications by filling in forms and making menu selections. Forms combined with menus are called frames. Frames combine the power of forms and the simplicity of menu-driven systems.
5. An application is organized as a hierarchy of frames. The user's selection of menu items determines the operations performed and the order in which frames are displayed.
6. Users specify custom operations through INGRES's fourth-generation development tool, the operation specification language (OSL).
7. Users can include programs written in conventional languages through INGRES/EQUEL.
8. Users can allow INGRES/REPORTS to select the appropriate report type or they can choose another.[2]

These fourth-generation systems encourage the development of applications without recourse to conventional programming. The choices that have been made in designing the user interface are intended to increase the accessibility of information stored in the computer.

In the near future, computer designers would like to have a natural language interface that would allow the user to communicate with the machine using everyday language. Some natural language interfaces are in use but they are limited in flexibility. They must first learn the pronunciation of a particular user and can only understand that person. These programs enable a person who cannot use a keyboard to control a computer.

In *The Cognitive Computer,* Roger Schank argued that natural language understanding and intelligent assistant programs will eliminate many of the obstacles to computer use by the average person. No longer would a user need to learn special commands to obtain information from a computer. Speech is a nearly universal human characteristic and a natural language interface would make computer information available to all. However, the need for information processing is not at this point nearly so universal. It may become easier to access computers than it is to read a book, yet the desire to become actively involved with information retrieval and analysis may be as limited by necessity or social fashion as the desire to become fully literate. Many functionally literate adults show great reticence when they find themselves in a university library with its arrays of books. Similar customs could easily come to surround the use of computer tools and databases.

We expect computers to be used by all sectors of our society. However, these expectations must be tempered by the existence in our society of audiences or publics with widely differing information needs and uses. When television was first widely introduced, many writers predicted it would bring high culture to the masses and change both teaching and education. Instead, for a variety of reasons, television became the "vast wasteland," a purveyor of visual information of eclectic content and quality. Repeated attempts to provide highbrow television, including the recent CBS Arts cable network, have met with failure. Educational television has made little headway beyond selected areas of institutional training. This is not to say that an audience for quality TV programming does not exist, but rather that this audience is much smaller than anticipated. Similarly, the number of people who will become active computer users may not be as large as we anticipate.

Computer information is of immediate importance and use to professionals and elite decision makers. For them, the information environment is a rapidly developing reality. Professionals learn the scope of this new environment through development seminars such as those offered by Control Data's Institute for Advanced Technology:

- Data Communications
- Data Base Management
- EDP Operations
- Software Engineering
- CAD/CAM
- Personal Computer
- Office Automation/Word Processing
- Management/Supervisory Development
- Marketing and Sales
- Secretarial/Administrative Assistant

The Institute for Advanced Technology has presented seminars in these areas to more than 100,000 professionals from more than 250 companies and institutions. Similar seminars are conducted by a number of computer education service companies. But it must be recalled that these seminars are for people for whom information was already important before the widespread use of computers.

The impact of the information environment in the workplace is only beginning and may diverge significantly from expectations, based upon what has happened in elite circles. The use of computers, databases, and electronic conferences by professionals and businessmen has followed their interests and modes of work. These highly trained individuals have frequently been allowed a high degree of freedom and flexibility in pursuing their work; this has extended to their use of computers. But it does not follow that the same freedom and flexibility will be allowed to average white-collar workers when they use computers.

Despite the possibilities for work decentralization and telecommuting, most white-collar workers in banks, insurance companies, and corporate offices have continued in established work patterns. In certain respects, however, the office worker's job has changed.

> Instead of using documents, reports, filing cards and forms the office worker now sits at his VDU [video display unit] screen entering data, following programmed procedures and watching the results. For this he has to learn how to handle the system, i.e., the dialog commands and data formats. A great part of the experience he had with the office procedures he performed before is not important any more. The procedures are incorporated in the programs he's working with. The remaining work processes of data preparation and interpretation get further standardised and formalised.[3]

In other respects, the tasks performed by the office worker remain the same. For widespread decentralization and telecommuting, a significant redefinition of the status and work of white-collar clerical staff would have to occur. As this might involve a loss of status and benefits as easily as an improvement, many vested interests oppose this change.

Beyond the elites and the white-collar groups, the impact of the information environment may prove to be negative, at least in the near term. Though educators often stress the general value of information, its actual value must be related to specific situations. The computer is a storehouse of specialized technical information, and this may be of little use to the nonspecialist. Many blue-collar workers will have computers at home, as they have televisions and telephones, but this will not change the realities of blue-collar work. The automation of factories and use of robots may benefit society generally, but it is often seen as a threat by older workers. Some workers can retrain for new jobs but many lack the educational skills required. From the blue-collar perspective, the control of computers and automation is largely a white-collar and professional affair.

User Roles and Computer Environments

As the information environment takes on a tangible form, a variety of user roles have developed. These roles are usually related to the various contexts in which computers are widely used—educational, professional, institutional, and home. In these contexts, different psychological and social expectations surround computers. In the classroom, for example, children are presented with computers for play and instruction. The user role children take on may have less to do with computers than with their own developmental needs: "Computers, as marginal objects on the boundary between the physical and the psychological, force thinking about matter, life, and mind. Children use them to build theories about the animate and the inanimate and to develop their ideas about thought itself."[4]

Similarly, the role of the hacker may have less to do with computer education than with the need to demonstrate mastery over a stealthy opponent: "Most hackers are young men for whom at a very early age mastery became highly charged, emotional, colored by a particular desire for perfection, and focused on triumph over things. Their pleasure is in manipulating and mastering their chosen object, in proving themselves with it."[5] Psychologically, the user's role can reflect his or her sense of self. Not only children and hackers display their competence and mastery of the machine through programming. Professional programmers may take great pride in their structured and efficient top-down programs. In contrast, the novice user's computer-phobia or fear of programming may reflect a fear of appearing incompetent before peers.

In addition to psychological factors, user roles are affected by the software environment and group expectations. Systems that are user-friendly may draw a very different response than systems that are user-hostile. The end user at a mainframe terminal must learn to deal with arcane protocols and weak documentation. The difficulty of using these systems supports the high status of those who can figure them out and gives such people an incentive for limiting access to the computer. The personal computer user, on the other hand, has more control over both machine and software and may come to find the restrictions of the mainframe environment irritating. The difference between these two computer environments can lead to confusion and frustration.

In the institutional settings where mainframe use predominates, user roles range from the active involvement in system design of the professional programmer to the more passive role of the clerical user. While the clerical staff are expected to input and process data, they are not expected to program. In this, they are users of a system designed by others:

> The system's behaviour and through it the surrounding *work organisation* is thus determined by the systems designers and programmers. Users normally only get some minimal information about the system. In many companies it is common to give them a short introduction in a training session of 2–3 hours at the terminal. After that they certainly do not understand how it works or how to recover from problematic situations in dialog. Their own role has been defined without them being able to exercise much influence, but nevertheless they have to conform to it.[6]

In contrast to the knowledge and autonomy enjoyed by the professional programmer, the clerical user's role is not far different from that of a machine operator in a factory. Even though the work environment is white collar, the clerical user may share the machine operator's feelings of isolation, powerlessness, and alienation.

The institutional mainframe culture is usually focused on a computer center or department that establishes guidelines for computer use and provides all aspects of support for the system. Because for many years computing time was a scarce resource in any institution, the prevailing norms in computer centers emphasized saving computer time and limiting access to the computer. These norms found a natural resonance in the obscurantist or mysterious attitude and confusing jargon of many computer specialists. As a result, many users came to see the mainframe as an inaccessible machine surrounded by a cryptic priesthood.

In contrast to the professional culture of programmers or the institutional mainframe culture, the fullest expression of a popular computer culture is found in the roles of personal computer users. In the last decade, a new culture arose around the personal computer and transformed the institutional computer environment. In one sense, beyond small university and research institute circles, a popular computer culture did not exist before the development and spread of personal computers. In the creation of the personal computer, the interplay of cultural vision and hardware/software development produced a number of innovations—the home computer, the user group, spreadsheets and word processing, the computer magazine and computer fair, the bulletin board, the user-friendly software environment, and the laptop machine. These cultural elements are commmonplace today, yet in large measure they did not exist in 1975.

Computer User Groups

The proliferation of user groups was one of the side effects of the spread of personal computers. User groups are similar to other special interest clubs. The first microcomputers were poorly documented and little software existed, so user groups came into existence to remedy these shortcomings. In turn, user-group evaluations and criticisms influenced the subsequent development of computers. A notable example was the Homebrew Computer Club in the San Francisco Bay area:

> Homebrew was a respected critic of microcomputer products. The Homebrewers were sharp, and could spot shoddy merchandise and items that were difficult to maintain. They blew the whistle on faulty equipment and meted out praise for solid engineering and convivial technologies. Homebrewers soon developed the power to make or break new companies. . . . Homebrew encouraged the conviction that computers should be used for and not against people.[7]

Although the difficulties posed by the first personal computers have been solved, the new user still finds problems that cause the machine or program to crash, and such information is often passed on to the user group. Computer clubs provide speakers and workshops so new hardware and software can be demonstrated. The more experienced users in a group can provide assistance during question-and-answer sessions. The meetings also provide occasions for anecdotes and digressions that pass on the folklore of the computing world. Special interest groups focusing on a particular subject such as desktop publishing or spreadsheets are sometimes formed.

Most of the information presented at a user-group meeting could be acquired from books or magazines, but learning the talk that goes with personal computers requires face to face sharing and participation with other computer users. This verbal interaction is sometimes found at computer stores, but the best opportunities for conversation about computers are at user-group meetings and computer shows. On these occasions, neophytes can learn from experts with some degree of equality and conviviality. Academic computer science courses provide another avenue for learning about computers, but they are more focused on programming and theory. The information acquired in academic courses leads to a professional expertise different from the computer lore learned in user clubs.

The excitement, adventure, and exchange of technical details and advice that surrounded the first microcomputers are being replaced by an established personal computer business. The corporate user expects a computer and software that will work right out of the box and require only a brief orientation. For many users, the computer is a tool that can be used without special technical expertise or reliance on a user group. For those with a technical bent, user groups remain a valuable resource. As the computer culture evolves, we can expect a continuing differentiation among users with differing technical and software interests.

Computer companies have shown great ambivalence about meeting the support needs of personal computer users, and users in turn hesitate to buy unsupported and unfamiliar machines. Some large computer manufacturers have been notably unsuccessful in the PC marketplace. The dominance of MS-DOS and Apple machines is partly a reflection of company support. But it is also a reflection of the support provided for these machines by user groups, magazines, software companies, and add-on manufacturers. Both IBM and Apple have introduced new models and upgrades positioned for sales rather than compatibility with earlier models. The personal computer user continually faces the problem of obsolete or orphan technology, with an unlimited budget for the latest hardware and software being the only real solution.

The Software Environment

We now recognize that the full utilization of computers rests on the software available to the user. The rapid development of personal computer software in the last decade has changed both the user's relationship to the machine and the machine's potential uses. With line-driven operating systems such as CPM and MS-DOS that were modeled on mainframe systems, the user had to know a set of commands to make the computer work. The commands were used to format disks, copy files, launch applications, check memory, and perform other routine tasks. Each word processing or spreadsheet application, in turn, had its own set of commands, which were usually different from those of the operating system.

Over time, the preferred end-user interface has evolved toward a standardized menu- or icon-driven environment that makes the operating system almost invisible. Choices selected from a menu with a keystroke or click of a mouse move the user's attention from the details of the machine to the software tools being used. The machine details and its programming are left to the software designers. Users need only be concerned with the software required for their specific purposes. The availability of user-friendly software for personal computers has created a demand for a similar software environment for all computers and is thus changing the institutional mainframe environment.

The proliferation and standardization of software has extended the range of personal computer applications. A recent software review for the IBM PC listed 1,500 programs in the following categories:

Application software
Integrated applications
Business management
Word processing
Financial applications
Spreadsheets
Job-specific applications
Data management
Education
Communications
Personal management
Graphics
Entertainment
Accounting
System software
Operating systems
Utilities
Languages

The wide range of custom application software has made the personal computer a flexible tool in both home and business environments. Flexibility has been enhanced with desk accessory and utility programs that allow the computer to be used as a notepad, appointment calendar, phone directory, or calculator. These minor programs create a familiar desktop environment for the user.

The emergence of desktop publishing as an important personal computer application is an excellent example of the unanticipated changes that can result when computers are readily available. This type of application was uncommon in the mainframe milieu because computer resources were too valuable for such relatively trivial uses. Mainframe resources were used for book and newspaper publishing, but applications such as newsletters were on too small a scale for these publishing systems. A personal computer with desktop publishing software and a laser printer turned out to be the right combination for small publishing projects. As a result, desktop publishing has developed as a major personal and business application.

The use of graphics and digitized images in desktop publishing also reflects an unanticipated use for the microcomputer. Graphics packages on mainframes, although appropriate for engineering or computer-aided design, were not suited to the illustration of reports. With the microcomputer, many graphics packages, libraries of designs, and fonts are available to use in reports, newsletters, and magazines. The cutting, pasting, and resizing techniques and the screen-oriented "what-you-see-is-what-you-get" system used in desktop publishing software provide a flexibility in graphic design that is quickly mastered by the user.

As personal computers have become commonplace, programmers have created many small-scale applications. For instance, software packages for sailboat navigation or amateur astronomy rely on computer graphics applied to a small body of knowledge. The maps and coordinate systems used in navigation and astronomy are not new information, but placing these systems on a personal computer allows the user to establish course longitude and latitude or locate star positions with ease. The astronomer can follow the motions of the stars in the heavens either forward or backward in time. This graphic presentation of information is a considerable plus for the amateur observer or navigator. Other small-scale applications assist the user with income tax returns or prepare menus that conform to a diet regimen. The possibilities for small applications have proven to be quite broad.

Computer Magazines

The role of magazines as a source of information and support in the computer culture is significant. One need only compare the newsletter of an institutional computer center with *BYTE, PC World, Macworld,* or *MacUser* to see the difference. Computer center newsletters provide technical information on system protocols, terminal locations, problems and fixes, and application packages; but despite recent interest in making mainframe computers more accessible, the newsletters remain sketchy and forbidding to the uninitiated. Computer magazines, in contrast, come in all levels of technical sophistication and reflect a broad range of user interests. Because magazines are often devoted to a particular family of computers, they can focus at length on reviews of the operating system, software, peripheral devices, and communications. New hardware and software are introduced and relevant major developments are discussed. Review articles compare several software packages of the same type—spreadsheets, for example—to indicate strengths and weaknesses. By reading these articles, the user learns not only about the specific software but also about spreadsheet structure and use. Computer center newsletters seldom provide this kind of information.

Computer magazines are, in their way, as important for the personal computer culture as the machines are. The computer owner who reads no computer magazines is at a disadvantage in following the continuing evolution of the computer. The combination of machine and magazine has a synergistic effect; in fact, the combination of several machines and magazines may increase this effect by extending the user's involvement and time with computers. Albeit with some journalistic exaggeration, the "Chaos Manor" column in *BYTE* magazine provides evidence of this effect. The author has numerous computers and unlimited software packages at Chaos Manor. He is continually upgrading his various systems, comparing different operating systems, fixing bugs, trying out new software, writing columns for computer magazines, and attending computer conferences. His wife, children, and friends also participate in this nonstop play with computers. Given the author's total immersion in computing, his asides in the column highlight the computer lifestyle.

Most users have not caught up with Chaos Manor and probably wouldn't want to. But users can participate in a community with those who have similar machines and software. The positive role of magazines and user groups is highlighted when a company fails. When Osborne Computer Company went into bankruptcy and *Portable Companion* ceased publication, Osborne users found themselves out in the cold. Portable computer pioneers in 1981–1982, they suddenly became owners of obsolete equipment. Feeling betrayed and disillusioned, no longer mentioned in the magazines except in terms of failure, Osborne owners turned for support to their user groups and especially to the First Osborne Group (FOG). FOG membership grew rapidly and the *FOGHORN* newsletter took over many of the information functions of *Portable Companion*. The FOG public domain software library, contributed by FOG members, provided users with various utilities and patches for

Osborne software. *FOGHORN* served as an outlet for manufacturers providing hardware and repairs for the Osborne. Alongside the manufacturers, magazines and user groups help to support the atmosphere of optimism and excitement that sustains the computer culture.

Bulletin Boards and Information Services

Another facet of the information culture has emerged around the use of bulletin boards and online information services. User-operated bulletin boards are culturally different from online database services. In many respects, bulletin boards are less uniform and conventional. Running a gamut from boards that focus on specific machines or operating systems to fantasy and adult interests, they vary greatly in structure and content. In contrast with commercial information services, the personal element is present both in language and in references to the board operator, or sysop. As a result, the bulletin board user may have a greater sense of making online contact and participating in an online community. This is reinforced by links between the bulletin boards and user groups in a particular locale. Users are told about software they can download and telephone numbers of interesting boards are exchanged at group meetings. Bulletin boards have also been associated with the communication of quasilegal and illegal information, pirated software, and restricted computer entry codes that are used by computer hackers. The legal controversy surrounding such information and the arrest of some bulletin board operators have clouded the future role of bulletin boards. The spread of destructive virus programs in software downloaded from bulletin boards has added to the controversy.

Bulletin boards do not usually charge a fee, and users can sample the boards in their area. In contrast, online database services usually have a substantial hourly connect charge and are therefore approached with more consideration of cost. Two different routes are open to information service users. First, they can subscribe to a general information service such as CompuServe, The Source, or Prodigy. At fairly modest rates, these services provide a wide variety of information on many subjects as well as the facility for online dialogs, mail, electronic publishing, online conferences, and shopping. Users of The Source, for example, can choose among the following major categories:

- Communications
- Business and Investment
- News and Sports
- Consumer Services
- Games and Entertainment

- Travel Services
- Publishing on The Source

Information can be uploaded from personal computers and downloaded from The Source. Users are allotted files on The Source for a variety of communication and information storage purposes. CompuServe, Prodigy, and other general information vendors provide similar services.

Second, the database user with more specialized information needs will begin with the selection of an appropriate information service and of software to facilitate access and reduce online costs. A variety of services provide literature citations and abstracts, topic research and document copies, and financial and time series data from a range of specialized databases. Some of the major services are

- General—Dialog/Knowledge Index, BRS/BRS After Dark, Delphi, SDC Orbit
- Financial—Dow Jones News/Retrieval, ADP, IDC, I. P. Sharp, Wharton, Predicasts, Data Courier
- Newsletters—NewsNet
- Medical—Medlars, Pharmaceutical News Index
- Legal—Lexis

Access to specialized databases is often gained through a general information service company such as Dialog. Database vendors initially dealt with an institutional clientele, and search charges were expensive. With the spread of personal computers, databases have been made available to a wider public, and new services (for example, Knowledge Index and BRS After Dark) at less expensive rates have been created. Because of the high online costs of a search, several software packages have been developed to allow the user to prepare a search offline. Once online, information found in the search is downloaded for storage and later reading. These procedures reduce online time and thereby the cost of using the information service.

Electronic Mail and Online Conferences

Across private and public networks, electronic mail is becoming an important new avenue for communication. Messages that used to be sent by phone, memo, or mail have been moved to electronic mail systems. These systems speed the transmission of routine communications, but also create a channel for more unusual messages. This has led to the formulation of a new etiquette for electronic mail. It has been suggested that messages should be brief, clear, and to the point. Aside from short general announcements, mail should be addressed to specific recipients. Junk mail, chain letters, gossip, and obscenities are proscribed. Given the essentially public nature of electronic mail networks, controversial statements that might be misunderstood are to be avoided. However, as with print mail, these rules regulating electronic mail may not always be followed.

For broader inter-user dialog and open discussion, online conferences are the preferred venue. Electronic conferences share some of the community characteristics of bulletin boards. The online conference format was developed by Murray Turoff in 1971 for the U.S. Office of Emergency Preparedness. With the computerized system: "groups of people–many of whom could never be brought together in the same place at the same time–could easily use this centralized information exchange to 'discuss' proposals and ideas. At any time of day or night, discussion-group members could use a computer terminal to contact the system. Once online, they could read all the comments made by all other members and add comments of their own."[8] Computerized conferences can take a variety of forms including a focused lecture/ seminar, a free-form discussion, an unstructured encounter, or a highly structured question-and-answer session.

According to study findings reported in *The Network Nation,* Starr Roxanne Hiltz and Murray Turoff found several changes in user behavior that emerge during online conferences. Many participants expressed some awkwardness in their first messages in a conference. This was soon replaced, for some, by a tendency toward lengthy proclamations. It became necessary to place a limit on the length of comments. As conferences evolved, participants often noted shortcomings in the discussion, but continued to participate. Online conferences have become a standard feature of general information networks such as The Source and *BYTE* magazine's BIX network. Conferences usually focus on a special interest or topic, and network subscribers are free to join and comment. In institutional settings, participation in a conference and access to the discussion are often restricted for reasons of efficiency and security. Along with bulletin boards and electronic mail, the electronic conference is one of the new communication frameworks developing in the information culture.

The Computer and the Arts

The computer is having an important impact in many spheres of artistic activity. Using traditional artistic technology, the production of artwork required considerable skill in materials preparation, drawing, handling of color, and finishing. Similarly, the production of accomplished music required years of training on acoustic instruments. In the nineteenth century, new mechanical and chemical techniques were applied to the reproduction of images and sounds. The invention of photography allowed the rapid capture and reproduction of images. Punched-paper control of mechanically driven musical instruments, as seen in the player piano, provided a means for the reproduction of musical performances. The invention of the phonograph allowed electronic recording and reproduction of musical performance taken from acoustic instruments. In many respects, the application of the computer to the arts is a continuation of these earlier technological innovations in the recording and reproduction of images and sounds.

With computer technology, images, sounds, or movements can be created, digitally captured or scanned from existing sources, stored, altered, and reproduced. Electronic musical instrument companies have designed custom microprocessors for the production and synthesis of digital sound. The musical instrument digital interface (MIDI) is being incorporated into most new electronic instruments, synthesizers, and computers. Using the available music software with a synthesizer, composers can generate, record, rearrange, and edit layers of sound. The emphasis in composition shifts from the production of sound using traditional acoustic instruments to the control of a complex electronic masterboard that interfaces to a variety of sound synthesizers.

Driven by commercial film animation and special effects companies, visual image processing is moving along similar lines. Interactive three-dimensional graphics workstations have been designed for animation work and are being adapted for the broader image processing market. Animators or engineers can use these workstations to create images with a number of layers; control color, shading, and lighting; and add motion and rotation. Many of these effects were commercially developed at great cost for use in motion pictures such as *Star Wars* and *Tron*. With the interactive graphics workstation, the cost of three-dimensional image processing is falling sharply and is thus available to a broad group of artists, designers, and engineers.

There are several ways in which the computer-enhanced artistic environment can be used. First, an image may be drawn or music may be produced on the computer, or the computer may be programmed to do these things. In either case, the computer becomes an artistic medium. Second, an existing image or sound may be input and processed by the computer. The computer translates and alters the input, thus changing it from one medium to another. Third, the computer can be used in conjunction with other electronic media to produce an artistic piece. In this instance, the computer is part of an artistic system. Fourth, the computer can be used to coordinate, order, and control a variety of electronic input media to produce a finished artistic product. Sharing a common digital interface, multimedia presentations combining sound, image, and movement can be created.

Several questions should be considered in looking at the various artistic products issuing from the computer-enhanced environment. In what substantive or qualitative ways are computer artworks different from those produced with traditional media? How is the traditional artwork changed in its conversion to an electronic environment? How does the nature of electronic digital media change the concerns and objectives of the artist? How do the storage and exact reproduction of electronic artworks affect the distinction between an original and a reproduction? Can the storage and preprogrammed features of computers lead to the nearly automatic production of art by novices?

In certain senses, these questions have already been answered. Since the beginning of this century, artistic production has moved steadily away from individual craft work toward mass production for the popular media. Film, musical recording, radio, and television share storage and reproduction characteristics similar to those of electronic computer art. The mass media have readily incorporated the new elements of computer enhancement, from computer-generated graphics to synthesized music. Media productions, including those enhanced by computer, are readily understood and appreciated by the public. Popular artists using electronic media are highly regarded. The original electronic creation and its reproduction are given equal weight, though the audience may regard the experiences in slightly different terms. As the media for reproduction of images and sounds improve in fidelity, they become a substitute for live performance.

The qualitative difference of electronic art from pre-electronic art is not easily stated. By examining the representations of the inner structure of the computer drawn by Robert Tinney, a cover artist for BYTE magazine, we can glimpse the difference. In Tinney's drawings of the digital world, the data of our "real" world are reproduced in a miniaturized, repetitive, hierarchical, and compartmentalized structure. This parallel universe in the computer mirrors our world and can endlessly be altered according to program in exactly structured variations. The artistic works of earlier technologies also mirrored our world but were not as readily transformed or subject to minute variation at the push of a button. In the past, art and its object remained relatively stable; with electronic media, transformation is the keynote.

In the last decade, the computer culture has evolved rapidly from the institutional arrangements surrounding mainframes and minicomputers to the new environment surrounding personal computers. It is expected that in the next two decades computers will become as ubiquitous and commonplace as telephones. The user will apply no more special attention to use these devices than we bring to our use of the telephone. Should we expect, then, that a distinctive computer culture will disappear? Certainly, a computer culture will exist among those technically involved with the machines and among other computer enthusiasts. Furthermore, we can expect a general social change resulting from the effects of the new information environment. This may be expressed in an increasingly procedural and rationalized view of problems and their solutions and in a reliance on numerous large and small databases. This social change has already affected our major institutions and will achieve a general impact in the next generation through our educational system. It is not that the computer culture will disappear, but that the larger culture will come to share many of its characteristics.

Notes

1. Sholom Weiss and Casimir Kulikowski, *A Practical Guide to Designing Expert Systems* (Totowa, New Jersey: Rowman and Allanheld, 1984), p. 159.

2. Selected from Relational Technology, Inc., INGRES/APPLICATIONS, INGRES/FORMS, and INGRES/REPORTS brochures, 1985. Also see Michael Stonebraker, ed., *The INGRES Papers* (Reading, Massachusetts: Addison-Wesley, 1986).

3. Susanne Maass, "Why Systems Transparency," in Thomas Green, Stephen Payne, and Gerritt van der Veer, eds., *The Psychology of Computer Use* (New York: Academic Press, 1983), p. 20.

4. Sherry Turkle, *The Second Self* (New York: Simon & Schuster, 1984), p. 31.

5. *Ibid.*, p. 201.

6. Susanne Maass, "Why Systems Transparency," p. 20.

7. Paul Freiberger and Michael Swaine, *Fire in the Valley* (Berkeley, California: Osborne/McGraw-Hill, 1984), p. 108.

8. Alfred Glossbrenner, *The Complete Handbook of Personal Computer Communications* (New York: St. Martin's Press, 1983), p. 209.

Selected Bibliography

Bolter, J. David. *Turing's Man* (Chapel Hill: University of North Carolina Press, 1984).

Carroll, John M., ed. *Interfacing Thought* (Cambridge, Massachusetts: The MIT Press, 1987).

Date, C. J. *A Guide to INGRES* (Reading, Massachusetts: Addison-Wesley, 1987).

Freiberger, Paul, and Michael Swaine. *Fire in the Valley* (Berkeley, California: Osborne/McGraw-Hill, 1984).

Glossbrenner, Alfred. *The Complete Handbook of Personal Computer Communications* (New York: St. Martin's Press, 1983).

Hiltz, Starr Roxanne. *Online Communities* (Norwood, New Jersey: Ablex Publishing, 1984).

Hiltz, Starr Roxanne, and Murray Turoff. *The Network Nation* (Reading, Massachusetts: Addison-Wesley, 1978).

Kearsley, Greg. *Online Help Systems* (Norwood, New Jersey: Ablex Publishing, 1988).

Lammers, Susan. *Programmers at Work* (Redmond, Washington: Microsoft Press, 1986).

Levy, Steven. *Hackers* (Garden City, New York: Doubleday, 1984).

Maass, Susanne. "Why Systems Transparency." In Thomas Green, Stephen Payne, and Gerritt van der Veer, eds. *The Psychology of Computer Use* (New York: Academic Press, 1983).

McCorduck, Pamela. *The Universal Machine* (New York: McGraw-Hill, 1985).

Nickerson, Raymond S. *Using Computers* (Cambridge, Massachusetts: The MIT Press, 1986).

Norman, Donald A., and Stephen W. Draper, eds. *User Centered System Design* (Hillsdale, New Jersey: Lawrence Erlbaum Associates, 1986).

Pagels, Heinz R. *Computer Culture* (New York: New York Academy of Sciences, 1984).

Price, Don K. *The Scientific Estate* (Cambridge, Massachusetts: Harvard University Press, 1965).

Schank, Roger C. *The Cognitive Computer* (Reading, Massachusetts: Addison-Wesley, 1984).

Stonebraker, Michael, ed. *The INGRES Papers* (Reading, Massachusetts: Addison-Wesley, 1986).

Turkle, Sherry. *The Second Self* (New York: Simon & Schuster, 1984).

Weiss, Sholom, and Casimir Kulikowski. *A Practical Guide to Designing Expert Systems* (Totowa, New Jersey: Rowman and Allanheld, 1984).

Computers
in Organizations

Since the 1970s, we have grown accustomed to the ready presence of computers; we number the machines not in thousands, but millions. The large number of machines and their diverse uses have altered the course of computerization. As late as 1968, there were only 50,000 installed computers in the United States, 3,000 in Great Britain, and 5,000 in West Germany. These were the mainframe variety of that period—they were expensive and cumbersome. Such installations required careful preliminary planning, customized software, and extensive staff training. As computers have changed in the last decades, becoming less expensive and more user-friendly, planning for computerization has become easier. However, in all institutions various arrangements have evolved to provide a framework for the use of computers.

Over the years, a number of concerns have shaped the organizational framework surrounding computers:

1. What computers are necessary to remain competitive with other organizations?
2. What software is required?
3. In what part of the organization should computers and related equipment be placed?

As data processing (DP) departments developed, other questions emerged:

1. What is the relationship of the data processing department to other departments?

2. What information services should the DP department provide to
the organization?
3. Who should plan for new computers?

With the introduction of minicomputers and personal computers, new
issues were raised:

1. Who should plan for and who should control these new machines?
2. Should the new computing environment be centralized or decentralized?
3. What network could link the various machines?
4. How will the new computers change the organization?

As computer applications have changed with the advance of computer
technology, the impact on institutions has increased and become more
general. A series of discrete changes in organizations, associated first
with mainframe computing and later with minicomputers and personal
computers, have finally produced an organizational environment in
which computers and the rapid exchange of electronic information are
essential.

Organizations in the Information Society

There is an extensive literature on organizations in industrial society.
With computers, the form of modern organizations is changing. Beginning
with a description of the post-1950 organization, we can trace some
of the changes that have occurred. Modern organizations before the
introduction of computers had many of the following characteristics:

1. Centralized command structure
2. Hierarchical department organization (the organization chart) and
task specialization
3. Mechanical office technology and large clerical staff
4. Paper records and files processed by departments
5. Planning and decision making by departments (de facto departmental autonomy)

In the first stages of computerization in the 1950s and 1960s, the
computer was primarily seen as a substitute for data processing by the
departments and a labor-saving device. The basic financial, billing,
accounting, and inventory records were to be transferred to the computer.
The systems were designed so data would move from the departments
to a centralized recording and computing facility that provided data

processing services for the entire organization. It was anticipated that the services of many of the clerical staff would no longer be required, but this seldom occurred in reality.

The difficulties in the early years of computerization resulted from a number of factors, some of which could not be foreseen at the time. In 1969, Michael Rose, an English sociologist, described the pitfalls of the computerization process in his book *Computers, Managers, and Society*.[1] In planning for computerization, organizations faced a number of new tasks. They had to evaluate their data processing requirements and select the right computer system from among the competing vendors. Before the equipment was installed, a data processing department had to be created and the clerical staff had to be prepared for the transition from paper to electronic record keeping. Once the computers were in place, the software had to be customized to meet the needs of the organization. Planning for a computer system usually took several months, and the installation and debugging of the system often required several more.

The computerization process could lag a year or two behind schedule. In the rush to embrace the new invention, organizations did not always assess their data processing needs clearly. Enthusiasm on the part of vendors and purchasers created expectations of computer performance that were beyond what the machines could deliver. At times, there was inadequate planning and preparation for the use of the new machines; then there were delays in delivery. The customization of the software took longer than anyone anticipated; in some cases it was never completed. There were administrative squabbles over the authority of the data processing department and reluctance on the part of the general staff to accept the new technology. The frequent disasters that occurred in the early years of computerization along with the orphan systems that resulted when computer manufacturers left the field made many companies wary of computers. To avoid these disasters and the costly investment in machines, other companies turned to independent data processing services.

Data and Information

As computer installations became more common in the 1960s, new uses were found for the data and information generated by data processing departments. The early image of the computer as an "electronic clerk" was replaced in the late 1960s and early 1970s as the concepts and uses of management information systems (MIS) were formulated. In MIS, the role of the computer was broadened from record keeping and data processing to providing information for planning and decision making.

Central to the concept of information systems is the recognition that data itself is not enough, that one may have a mountain of data and still have too little information. Managers and staff are deluged with memoranda, reports, and statistics. What must these contain to become useful information? There are several key characteristics of "generic" information: 1) accuracy, 2) timeliness, 3) completeness, 4) conciseness, 5) relevancy, and 6) accessibility.[2] To provide information that has these characteristics, the information system analysts must assess the information needs of the different parts of the organization and design a system that enhances the flow of information. The system design affects the kinds of data that are collected, how the data are structured and analyzed, and where the results are sent.

Information Systems and Organization Structure

The information systems perspective emphasizes the use of computers to provide information and support for managerial tasks and decisions, thus creating a decision support system. Data processing remains the main task of large EDP (electronic data processing) installations, but system managers are increasingly concerned with the information needs and strategy of the overall organization. This broader view is intended to remove obstacles to information flow and planning within the organizational hierarchy. In many instances, information is lost to management and staff because of departmentalization, lack of horizontal communication, and delays in communication between different levels of the organization. These obstacles hinder decision making, planning, and the evaluation of projects. By implementing an information systems strategy, organizations seek to use their computer data banks and networks to improve the flow of critical information.

In a 1974 collection of conference papers, *Strategic Planning for MIS,* the International Business Machines Corporation (IBM) offered an account of its own experience with information system planning. Initial computer use at IBM, as at other corporations, was directed toward specific data processing applications. In 1967, executive management mandated the creation of a unified information system for the entire company. Design objectives for the system architecture included the provision of functional information, information flow networks, data management, and standards development. The system architecture provided a logical information network for the company: "The network defined the major data bases and the business processes that would share data from those data bases. These logical groupings were termed 'information system centers.'"[3] Within this framework, information and data standards were established and information movement was planned to provide operational data to management. This, in turn, was intended to provide information for planning efforts to meet company objectives and to allow monitoring of the progress of company projects. The information system was also designed to chart its own efficiency and provide for expansion when necessary.

In 1967, recognizing the essential novelty of organizing and managing an information system, IBM established a System Science Institute (later renamed Information Systems Management Institute) to offer courses in system design and management. The institute currently offers thirty-eight courses in the following areas: 1) communications systems and systems management, 2) planning in the information systems environment, 3) protecting assets in the information systems environment, 4) management skills and professional development, 5) application development for information systems professionals and users, and 6) end-user computing and productivity. Through the systems institute seminars, IBM has made its experience with information systems an organizational model. Managerial teams from other corporations attend institute seminars to learn the techniques of information system planning. They return to their organizations to assess the particular information area they are concerned with and draft a plan following the IBM guidelines. When this has been completed, the managerial teams return to the institute seminar to present the draft plan and have it critiqued by the institute specialists. Although these plans are not necessarily implemented by each organization, the process helps managers recognize the key issues in planning for future changes in their organization's information system.

Designing Information Systems

Ideally, there are several stages in the design and implementation of integrated information systems. These stages include

1. Assessment of the information requirements of the organization
2. Design of a logical information network and system
3. Definition of data and information standards for the system
4. Test of the new system
5. Conversion to the new system

The design of the information system, although focused on information internal to an organization, must also consider information that may be acquired from external sources. As networks are established, it

Table 4.1
Areas of Information System Impact

Organization	*Group*	*Individual*
Formal or Visible		
Centralization/decentralization	Work group structure	Task content
Departmental tasks	Tasks	Autonomy
Operating procedures	Intra-group relationships	Recruitment needs
Communication networks		Retention
Monitoring		
Informal or Latent		
Power centers	Social group structure	Stress
Departmental cooperation or rivalry	Group norms	Status and power
Communication effectiveness	Attitudes	Attitudes
	Authority and leadership	Feelings
	Morale	

Source: John Abbott Worthley, *Managing Computers in Health Care: A Guide for Professionals* (Ann Arbor, Michigan: Health Administration Press, 1982), p. 106. Used with the permission of the publisher.

becomes fairly easy for a person in an automated office to access external databases and obtain information on competitors' actions. Further, as not all information is kept in electronic form, the information system should take into account the possible use of non-computer information resources.

In reality, the ideal system is tempered by the old habits and customs of information exchange in the organization. Information, after all, is also a source of power, and there are many opportunities for individuals in an organization to monopolize this resource. The information systems analyst is not operating in a neutral environment. Changes in the way information is collected, how it is analyzed, and where it is sent are matters of great concern to managers and staff. As an outsider, the systems analyst may have difficulty in obtaining information critical to a new design. If there is a feeling that information system reforms are not being handled in their best interest, managers and staff can obstruct or neglect the design put forward by the systems analyst.

A large number of formal and informal changes in both organization and work can result from a new information system (see Table 4.1). Formal changes in the work of individuals, groups, and departments often have latent consequences that change the status, power, and feelings of those involved. Even careful efforts to gain cooperation and understanding when planning an information system will not be able to anticipate all of the ramifications for the individual and the group.

The Data Processing Department

In many organizations, computer services are centralized in a data processing (DP) department. Originally established for accounting and record-keeping tasks, the data processing department has usually expanded to provide a variety of services to the organization including development of new systems, provision of information for planning, project tracking, evaluation of new equipment, and responsibility for computer networks in the organization. A variety of routine functions are also handled by this department, including software maintenance, account management, computer security, and user information. The staff of the data processing department include the DP managers, system analysts, programmers, and support staff. In a large organization, the staff are assigned to different tasks and projects, with some overseeing system operation and maintaining the system while others are assigned to new applications.

System Operation and Software Engineering

Routine system operation is the purview of the system administrator and the system operators. Behind every large-scale computer system, unseen by the users, lies a complex realm of administrative activity. Unlike a personal computer, a time-sharing network requires ongoing monitoring activity by the system operators. From the initial installation of the system through shakedown and routine operation, the system administrator and the operators must allocate network resources in ways that are particular to each organization.

During the installation phase, the system administrator must take the operating system provided by the vendor and use it to set the system and peripheral device defaults; directories and file structure; and individual user access rights, work space, and memory. The master file directory level of the operating system is not usually open to the end users, and changes in the system configuration can only be made by the system administrator. Once the system is in routine operation, the system operators monitor the status of the hardware, software, and peripherals; the activity of users; and the security of the system. They also deal with user requests and complaints. Unusual system events or problems are noted, and a system logbook is maintained by the operators. Regular system shutdown intervals are scheduled for hardware and software maintenance. An increase in the number of users or other increase in demand for system time may require changes in the system configuration and in each user's allocation of memory space.

Table 4.2
Programming Project Size and Complexity

Size of project	Level of complexity
Up to 1,000 lines	Trivial
1,000 to 10,000 lines	Simple
10,001 to 100,000 lines	Difficult
100,001 to 1,000,000 lines	Complex
1,000,001 to 10,000,000 lines	Nearly impossible
More than 10,000,000 lines	Absurd

Source: Edward Yourdon, *Managing the System Life Cycle,* 2e, © 1988, p. 2. Reprinted with permission of Prentice Hall, Inc., Englewood Cliffs, New Jersey.

A large percentage of the data processing staff time is devoted to programming and software maintenance. The software life cycle consists of five stages: 1) project specification, planning, and analysis; 2) design; 3) implementation; 4) testing; and 5) maintenance. The system vendor and independent software companies provide the operating system and large application packages. Programmers in an organization must customize and maintain this software as well as write smaller applications when required by the system users. Various authors have suggested different arrangements for an ideal programming team. Frederick Brooks, in *The Mythical Man-Month,* argues for the use of a small team under the direction of a chief programmer, with clerical support and a person assigned to program documentation.

With large projects, programming teams are assigned to write different parts of the program, and these program sections are integrated by other programmers assigned to system implementation and debugging in the later stages of the project. Yet, the sheer size of a programming project may defeat attempts at orderly software development and documentation. As Edward Yourdon has observed, as the number of lines of code to be written increases, the more complex the project becomes (see Table 4.2). Programming projects requiring more than 100,000 lines involve dozens of programmers over a span of years. Maintaining control and order as the project advances and programmers leave for other jobs is very difficult. For this reason, large programming projects evolve in unplanned directions, program sections escape documentation, and project completion deadlines recede into the future.

To assist programmers in software development and maintenance, software companies have created language toolboxes and utilities. Programmer's workbenches have been developed to link tools for program code development, debugging, and maintenance. Software companies are also creating tools for computer-assisted code development. Libraries of software modules are available to control screen input and output, graphics, file structure, and file management, and thus shorten the time needed to write and debug a program. System managers anticipate that further advances in computer-assisted software engineering (CASE) will help programmers ease the current backlog in program development and maintenance.

The introduction of fourth-generation languages and application generators has made it easier for end users to create some programs for reports, database query, and data analysis. In certain fourth-generation environments, these applications can be created simply by selecting desired items from a list of options offered by the application generator. However, system managers are concerned about the possible proliferation of nonstandard and undocumented programs in their systems and therefore do not wish to encourage extensive end-user programming. For optimized programs or nonstandard queries, the programming task remains with the professional system programmers.

In recent years, the established routines of data processing departments have been upset by corporate mergers and by demands for service from new computer users. The centralized control over computing enjoyed by the data processing department has also been weakened by the widespread introduction of microcomputers. William Synnott, chief information officer for the First National Bank of Boston, observes:

> As you move from centralized, big mainframe computers to decentralized minis and micros, the role of data processing is changing. First of all, it serves more as a corporate data base repository, whereby people go and get the data to put on their minis and micros or offload through high-level languages information they need for management support. So in one sense, you're serving as a sort of corporate data base repository. In another sense, you're running corporate systems, those things that will never be decentralized, because they're the bread and butter of your operation, and they spread across the corporation—like deposits and loans in a bank.[4]

In a sense, data processing departments are being pulled in several directions at once. Although different groups of computer users in an organization expect their needs to be given priority, the data processing department must confront its own resource limits. Information and databases of one organization may not match those of a new partner, and, similarly, within an organization the mainframe system may not fit with the popular microcomputers. These problems of system and information compatibility may be transitional ones, but they highlight the planning difficulties that confront the organization. If the data processing staff reacts defensively to this new situation the process of transition will be lengthened.

The Information Center

In some organizations, an information resource center has been established to handle the personal computer needs of the organization and to serve as a buffer between new users and the data processing department. These centers have taken a variety of forms. Sometimes companies use the centers to select, demonstrate, and support company approved computers or software and to facilitate user support groups. In others, the centers have run microcomputer training programs for the managers and staff. At times, DP or information center staff are available to provide support to users in preparing custom software applications.

With an information center, training experiences with personal computer hardware and software can become the basis for cooperation in integrating the computers into the company environment. The DP staff is made aware of the problems faced by the novice computer user. At the same time, some of the user demands for support and advice are shifted from the data processing department to the information center. Users are encouraged to become self-sufficient and disappointment with central DP is decreased.

Although considerable information processing can be done on microcomputers, larger computing tasks and large networks will continue to require the mainframe services of the data processing department. William Perry, in *The Micro-Mainframe Link: The Corporate Guide to Productive Use of the Microcomputer,* proposes that the data processing department rethink its role in the organization: "The mission of doing all of the computer processing is no longer valid. The central function must rethink what aspects of information processing are most effectively done centrally and what are most effectively done decentrally."[5] Perry describes four phases in the integration of microcomputers into the organization environment:

1. Experimentation phase—decentralization of some processing applications
2. Stand-alone phase—selection of user developed, maintained, and operated applications
3. Network terminal phase—elimination of data limitations
4. Workstation phase—elimination of processing limitations hardware/software limitations)[6]

Perry suggests that the data processing staff should lead the organization in planning for the integration of microcomputers with the existing computing system because most users cannot "devote full time to understanding and optimizing the use of information technology for the business."[7]

Unfortunately, in many organizations hostility has developed between the data processing department and the new personal computer users. When personal computers are not fully utilized, fail to perform as promised, or break down, the data processing department may adopt an "I told you so" attitude. Requests for information from end users may receive curt replies, and the micro-mainframe communication links may not be fully supported. A breakdown in communication between end users and the systems personnel may result.

This pattern of hostility did not originate with the personal computer. It can be traced back to earlier frustrations experienced by users of the data processing facilities. The data processing staff were often felt to be aloof and overly technical. Because of frequent processing backlogs, reports were usually late and response to special processing requests was almost out of the question. As the following example from McGraw-Hill Book Company illustrates, it was this situation that made the personal computer attractive:

> We had some special marketing reports which we wanted to use. The centralized systems group was not going to adjust the basic reports just because I needed them. In a way, you can not blame them because 50 to 60 percent of the divisions were able to use those reports. They can not go back and create new reports for other divisions, it does not make economic sense. With us being unhappy with the centralized group and not wanting to spend the money on time-sharing, we decided to go out and get our own Apple and start doing our reports. We figured we could tailor those reports to fill our needs. They were not reports that we really wanted to share with anybody else in the company because a lot of them were modeling and "what-if" situations. We did not feel they were for publication, but for divisional management use only.[8]

In another instance at McGraw-Hill, a new book marketing channel, an "electronic bookshelf" on the Apple Bulletin Board System, was developed on a personal computer and demonstrated to the marketing vice president. One of the developers noted: "I would have never had the energy to go through central data processing to develop this application; it would have taken at least 18 months. Ultimately, this application could justify being put on a time-sharing network, and I do not think doing this . . . would conflict with anything corporate

MIS is doing."[9] To overcome the negative climate that exists between central data processing and its clients, an initiative from the executive leaders of the organization may be necessary.

Information Resource Management

As the computing and information environment changes, many organizations are creating a new executive vice president position, the chief information officer (CIO), to oversee and plan all the different aspects of the new environment, including data processing, MIS planning, office automation, and communications. Although some data processing managers have been promoted to this position, the favored choice is a person with a strong background in management, planning, and overall knowledge of the organization. This choice is often made in an attempt to overcome some of the resistance to a person with an overly technical bent or a perceived special interest. By taking the view of the organization as a whole, the CIO can balance the computing interests and proposals of the various departments.

In line with the new importance of information resource management, the chief information officer is usually on an equal footing with the other main executives of the organization. To formulate an information strategy and integrate the information resources of a company across departmental lines, the CIO requires the cooperation and support of the top levels of management. Data processing and information system managers did not have such a broad mandate.

Among corporate executives, there is a growing recognition of the competitive significance of information: "In the past, most companies looked at information as an accounting kind of function or as a financial reporting function or what have you. There's a growing awareness that because you have this data base of information, you can use it for competitive and strategic advantage."[10] A key aspect of the chief information officer's assignment is creating a strategy for his or her organization to provide information services to its clientele that cannot be provided by competitors. Recent restructuring of financial institutions that have placed brokerage houses under the control of insurance companies (e.g., Bache with Prudential) or other financial organizations (e.g., Shearson/Lehman Brothers with American Express or Dean Witter with Sears) reflect this strategy. Financial institutions plan to market a broad range of services to their customers. From a personal computer or over the phone, they will be able to invest, pay bills, bank, or otherwise exercise cash management. Once the clientele becomes accustomed to these arrangements, the financial institutions will be assured of a loyal and dependent body of customers.

Networks

In order to achieve their financial and marketing strategies on a national or international scale and be able to evaluate and control the actions of their subsidiary units, corporations have created large networks that link the mainframes at headquarters with distributed minicomputers and office workstations. Through electronic mail, these systems allow direct communication between main office executives and the different managerial levels throughout the company. The system at the brokerage house E.F. Hutton is an excellent example of current developments.[11]

The information network at E.F. Hutton began with the linking of head office IBM 3080 and 3090 mainframes with regional office Data General Eclipse minicomputers in 1978. This system was expanded to the 400 worldwide branch offices in 1984 with the addition of Data General MV minicomputers running Comprehensive Electronic Office software. This system allowed distributed information processing at the different levels of the company and access to data in the central mainframes. Hutton stockbrokers, who must have current information on stock market activity, stock analysis, customer accounts, and buy and sell orders, had worked with dumb terminals for a decade. They are replacing the terminals with personal computers to have local processing, faster access to company data, run Lotus 1-2-3, and present stock data graphics. To enhance the decisions made by the brokers, the company is looking into expert systems that will alert brokers to significant market trends as they occur.

To complement the leased ground line computer network, E.F. Hutton has established a satellite communication network for broadcast transmission of voice and data to the offices. The satellite system is used for communications such as the "Morning Market Letter" that are sent to all E.F. Hutton locations. The information sent via satellite is encrypted to prevent spying.

The Hutton network is also being used to attract customers by making it possible for people with personal computers to link up with some of the resources available on the network. Customers can get quotes on securities, options, and market indexes; personal account information; access to investment research; and send electronic mail to their account executive. Customers pay a small monthly fee for this service.

With its network, E.F. Hutton management expects to be able to increase the productivity of its brokers by giving them a competitive advantage over brokers in other companies and by accelerating information flow within the company. However, as Hutton learned after pleading guilty to mail and wire fraud violations carried out using the branch information processing system, central accounting controls must be built into a financial transactions network. Branch managers were able to maintain zero or negative balances in their accounts and use the money for investments, an activity at variance with main office procedure.

As a result of the federal prosecution for fraud, Hutton has now centralized the auditing of its branches and reduced their financial independence. The information processing system was modified to control account draw-down and track Hutton's banking activities. The Hutton fraud, similar to the common individual practice of using the time delay between writing a check and the withdrawal of the funds from an account to cover any shortfall, was magnified by the power of the network and the sums of money being withdrawn from the accounts. Network designers did not see this potential abuse until after the fact.

Although many institutions are building their own networks, these do not necessarily contain all of the information needed by the institution. For external information, institutions rely on network information vendors such as DIALOG, BRS, or Dow Jones. The role of these information vendors has been expanding rapidly as large and small organizations come to rely on them for abstracts and data on their particular working environment. For example, to publicize the business databases that are available on DIALOG, a series of free "Know Your Market" seminars have been held. At these seminars, representatives of Data Courier, DIALOG, Disclosure, Business Research, and Predicasts present their relevant databases. Those in attendance are led through the fundamentals of online searching and some typical searches for product information. Although many users of an inhouse information network would not need to access an external information vendor, a gateway provides a means for those who do.

The Electronic Office

Increasingly, the office and desktop are the point of convergence for computing and information resources. With the movement of personal computers into the office environment, databases, network information, and computer analysis become proximate resources. The replacement of manual office equipment with terminals, personal computers, and printers often proceeds in chaotic fashion. The applications running on the computers, from word processing and spreadsheets to presentation graphics and project management, upset customary office procedures. College-educated staff are usually quick to assimilate and use statistical and planning techniques that have previously been the province of specialists. Office staff who are fluent in the use of computers find themselves in demand; others, not familiar with the new technology, may feel ignored.

With the demands for computers and new software coming from all parts of the organization, many companies have allowed departments to select from approved hardware (IBM, DEC, or Wang) and software (Lotus 1-2-3). As in the early years of mainframe computer installation, the vendors at times have oversold the capabilities of the personal computers. It was anticipated, for example, that some mode would be found to link the personal computers in local-area networks (LANs) so data and peripherals could be shared by several machines. At first, however, because of hardware or software incompatibilities, these networks were difficult to establish. Organizations are now more carefully considering which network infrastructure to establish and what hardware to place on the network.

As office groups have begun to use LAN-connected computers, new software for document processing, communication, and teamwork is being written. Document image processing systems make it possible for teams to create, edit, and store documents or reports. Similar systems can be used in architecture or engineering offices for drawings. Specialized groupware allows for the exchange of messages, group scheduling, conferences, project tracking, and other ways to enhance group productivity on the network. For professionals or salespeople who spend considerable time away from the office, groupware makes it possible to call in and keep up with group activities, file reports, and participate in conferences. With desktop publishing and presentation graphics, reports and project results can be effectively communicated to other groups in the organization. In time, more projects and teams will use local-area networks, and new forms of groupware will emerge.

The increasing automation of routine clerical work has created some anxiety among the less educated white-collar and clerical staff. Some employees have felt they would not be able to master the new machines or the complicated software. Others feared they would lose their jobs. In most cases, however, employees have been able to master the machines, and job loss has been handled through attrition or transfer. However, clerical workers have found work in the electronic environment to be more demanding and require more diligence than they were used to. Serious concerns have been expressed about the health consequences of prolonged exposure to the video display screen. Clerical employees, required to spend long hours entering data on a terminal, have complained of eye strain, headaches, backaches, and disorientation. They have also found long sessions on the terminals to be socially isolating. Some state health authorities have recommended that terminal sessions be limited to three hours.

Clerical employees have also raised concerns about the pace of work and the surveillance of workers in the automated environment. Though in the past work pace and supervision were controlled by the office manager, the clerical staff now feels the pace is set by the machine. This speed-up in paperwork is similar to the speed-up in manufacturing that accompanied the assembly line. The computer also allows a supervisor to monitor the work rate of the individual office worker. The clerical staff may feel that their customary time for breaks and talk when the manager is not around is threatened by this machine surveillance.

The fears and anxieties of the clerical staff may be alleviated in several ways. The information center can provide opportunites for the staff to train on the new equipment and familiarize themselves with the new system. Using staff input in planning for the new system will help in the redesign of jobs and tasks. Providing appropriate space, furniture, and lighting to allow both desk work and computer work will ameliorate some of the stress factors associated with the new systems.

Studies by Shoshana Zuboff have shown that the automation of the office environment is viewed differently by and has different consequences for clerical and professional groups in the office. College-educated designers, technical staff, analysts, and managers are not tied down to their workstations. For them, office automation provides new information and tools for design, analysis, and communication. The information system gives them better control of the organization and clerical staff and more autonomy in their own work. However, project records, mail, and conference discussions on computer networks also make the actions of managers and professionals more visible to their peers and superiors, and thus increase the pressure for on-the-job performance. Working in an information system environment, a manager may find it more difficult to hide delays or incompetence. Professionals may find that their customary autonomy and free discussion is being limited by new managerial concerns for efficiency, accountability, and information system security. The critical attitudes and negative stereotypes with which managers and professionals may view members of the other group can become more visible when captured in the electronic record. A new discretion in communication may be required to maintain existing areas of privacy and social distance between different office groups.

For the clerical staff, the computer or terminal requires the quick and careful performance of routine tasks. Their work pace can easily be monitored by supervisors. Constantly tending the machine, they are isolated from co-workers and may have less freedom than before. In the long term, new techniques like document image processing may eliminate many routine paperwork tasks, and the clerical staff will have to retrain for other work in the electronic office. As office automation takes hold, the anxieties and concerns of different staff groups reflect the changing nature of work in an information system environment.

System Security

As computers have come to play a central role in business and government, they have become the target of criminal activity and malicious mischief. Incidents of computer fraud, embezzlement, espionage, theft of programs or proprietary information, and vandalism have been widely reported in the media. Institutions in which computers are used have become increasingly security conscious and have taken a wide range of measures to physically protect and ensure the security and integrity of the information stored in their computers.

In the mainframe environment, hardware security was achieved by isolating the computer and limiting access to the machine. Plans were formulated to deal with disasters such as fires or floods, and separate backup systems at other sites were used to ensure the safety of large databases. In the case of a disaster, operations could be shifted to the backup site and continue without costly interruption.

User access to the mainframe system was controlled by assigning passwords and different levels of access to files and the operating system. As intrusion by outsiders has become a problem, companies have tried to make employees more careful with their passwords. Systems are monitored for repeated attempts to enter and these are reported to the system operators. However, as several embezzlement cases demonstrated, these controls were of little use when the perpetrator was on the programming staff or managed accounts on the system. Keeping outsiders from penetrating a computer system poses one set of problems. Keeping insiders honest or preventing a fired programmer from leaving behind a logic bomb that will destroy the file index poses a different set of problems.

With the spread of personal computers, it became fairly easy to steal both computers and software, which were often only locked in a room. The illegal copying of software also became a problem. Companies have responded by placing machines in locked brackets and training employees to be careful with floppy disks. However, personal computer hardware remains much more vulnerable to theft or damage than the more protected mainframe sites. When personal computers with modems became commonplace in the 1980s, the existing mainframe access security systems proved inadequate. The spread of networks and the increasing number of system access points have made it easier to break into computer systems. One group of Wisconsin hackers, the 414s, broke into more than sixty major computer installations through the national Telenet system before federal authorities stopped them. Because many hackers were teenagers, their penetration of computer systems was initially viewed as mischief more than crime. This tolerant attitude toward intruders is no longer widely held.

The success of hackers in obtaining passwords and gaining access to government and business computers through the networks prompted federal and state governments to pass laws penalizing this activity. Institutions responded by making their personnel more security conscious, by installing more elaborate password and call-back systems, and, to an extent, by the encryption of data. Encryption is usually reserved for sensitive financial or government information. Several encryption algorithms are available using either a single-key or double-key system. In single-key systems, a single private key is used to encrypt and decode. In double-key systems, a public key is used to encrypt and a private key to decode. The National Bureau of Standards and the National Security Agency have evaluated different encryption algorithms and until recently supported the Data Encryption Standard algorithm. This algorithm used sixteen repetitions of substitution and permutation to encrypt data. The cost of encrypting information has been decreasing, and the threat of tampering has led to more data encryption to protect the integrity of sensitive information.

Multiple levels of security may make it harder for the outsider to penetrate the system, but this approach is not as effective against fraud, embezzlement, and other security threats from within the organization. Programmers and other inside personnel have ample opportunities to embezzle funds within computer accounting systems. A variety of tactics will achieve this goal with a minimum of visibility. The electronic transfer of several million dollars to a Swiss bank was used in one well-known case. In another case, fractions of pennies from all of a bank's accounts were placed on a daily basis in an account created by the embezzler. These small amounts were not missed until the fraud was accidentally discovered. Similar cases of computer embezzlement may go unnoticed unless the auditing of the system accounts is very careful. Also, many computer crimes are not reported because companies do not want to reveal the weak points of their systems. As more and more valuable information resides in computers, we anticipate that more instances of computer fraud and embezzlement will occur.

Mischievous damage can be as great a problem for computer users as actual crime is for the institutions. The current threats to computer information, the virus programs evolved from the Trojan horse and logic bomb, have had a particularly chilling effect on the computer culture. Designed to reproduce contagiously through computer systems, virus and worm programs have infected new systems through files or software sent between machines, through software downloaded from bulletin boards, and from utility and shareware disks exchanged in user groups. Because a virus program can be designed to remain dormant for some time, it can unknowingly be spread when programs or files are moved between systems. The 1988 incident when a worm program entered more than 7,000 UNIX systems through the Internet network has highlighted the vulnerability of networked systems to intrusion. Although the worm program was not intended to be destructive, it tied up and disrupted a nationwide network of computers for more than 24 hours. A considerable amount of computer time was also lost while operators purged their systems.

As a result of virus threats, most users have become very cautious about introducing downloaded or free software into their systems. Vaccine programs to check for and eliminate viruses are being distributed, but such vaccines can only work against the usual viral program. Because new virus programs will be created, caution when exchanging programs and files is becoming the preferred course for computer users.

Though most computer security measures have focused on the systems within organizations, the global networking of computers has made it possible to monitor data flows once they move outside the secured boundary of the institution. U.S., European, and Russian intelligence agencies have invested heavily in computers to monitor international telecommunications. At the same time, businesses and governments are developing inexpensive encryption techniques to make this monitoring more difficult in the future.

At this time, computers, the information in them, and the networks are not secure. As new security measures are developed, new techniques for computer penetration and theft are created. Computer security analysts have recommended that organizations determine the areas of greatest importance and risk and concentrate their efforts on protecting those areas while accepting some loss in less important sections.

Innovation and Change

As we have seen, a number of institutional changes are associated with the introduction and use of computers in organizations. In our discussion, we have usually assumed that the process of computerization, if successfully carried out, leads to a more efficient and rational organization. A successful information system provides the tools for administrative guidance and control of the organization. At times, computers have been associated with new, highly innovative forms of organization. Rosabeth Moss Kanter, in *The Change Masters,* has described the emergence in the 1970s of corporations that met the challenge of competition through individual initiative and open communication. These companies were often in high-technology areas such as computers and integrated circuits, and their work forces were highly educated and flexible. Teamwork and high levels of participation have been achieved in these companies. Kanter suggests that these companies share a culture of enterprise and innovation that can serve as a model for the transformation of U.S. industry. The use of computers is central to the development of these high-technology organizations, but the culture of innovation rests upon a remodeling of managerial and work relations that goes far beyond the introduction of computers.

Many traditional organizations based on hierarchy, separation of departments, and industrial work rules resist the changes that would be necessary to become more flexible and innovative. In these cases, computers can reinforce the status quo in an organization: "For the most part, computers do not dramatically alter power relationships among people in organizations, nor do they dramatically alter the missions of organizations. Most often, computers tend to reinforce current power relationships and to improve the performance of existing operations."[12] In instances where institutional reform, change of leadership, or democratization is needed to meet the challenge of competition, innovative leaders and individuals may discover to their disappointment that computers can reinforce the existing organization. However, computers, as a new technology, are subtly changing the procedures of organizations and altering their operating environment. The extreme competition in this environment, as information is increasingly used for strategic advantage, may force traditional organizations to adopt new modes of work to survive.

Notes

1. Michael Rose, *Computers, Managers and Society* (Baltimore, Maryland: Penguin Books, 1969).

2. John A. Worthley, *Managing Computers in Health Care* (Ann Arbor, Michigan: Association of University Programs in Health Administration [AUPHA] Press, 1982), p. 43.

3. Ephraim McLean and John Soden, *Strategic Planning for MIS* (New York: John Wiley and Sons, 1977), p. 179.

4. Interview with William Synnott, *Computerworld,* May 13, 1985, p. ID/11.

5. William Perry, *The Micro-Mainframe Link: The Corporate Guide to Productive Use of the Microcomputer,* excerpted in *Computerworld,* June 24, 1985, p. ID/8.

6. *Ibid.,* pp. ID/8–ID/9.

7. *Ibid.,* p. ID/9.

8. James Cash, Jr., F. Warren McFarlan, and James McKenney, *Corporate Information Systems Management* (Homewood, Illinois: Richard Irwin, 1983), pp. 170, 172.

9. *Ibid.,* p. 174.

10. Interview with David Haskin, *Computerworld,* May 13, 1985, p. ID/14.

11. Alan Alper, "E.F. Hutton: MIS, end users unite to take on Wall Street," *Computerworld,* August 11, 1986, pp. 63–69.

12. Kenneth Kraemer, William Dutton, and Alana Northrop, *The Management of Information Systems* (New York: Columbia University Press, 1981), p. 343.

Selected Bibiography

Alper, Alan. "E.F. Hutton: MIS, end users unite to take on Wall Street." *Computerworld* (August 11, 1986): 63–69.

Brooks, Frederick P., Jr. *The Mythical Man-Month* (Reading, Massachusetts: Addison-Wesley, 1982).

Cash, James, Jr., F. Warren McFarlan, and James McKenney. *Corporate Information Systems Management* (Homewood, Illinois: Richard Irwin, 1983).

Garson, Barbara. *The Electronic Sweatshop* (New York: Simon & Schuster, 1988).

Interview with David Haskin. *Computerworld* (May 13, 1985): ID/14.

Interview with William Synnott. *Computerworld* (May 13, 1985): ID/11.

Kanter, Rosabeth Moss. *The Change Masters* (New York: Simon & Schuster, 1983).

Kopeck, Ronald F. *Micro to Mainframe Links* (Berkeley, California: Osborne/ McGraw-Hill, 1986).

Kraemer, Kenneth, William Dutton, and Alana Northrop. *The Management of Information Systems* (New York: Columbia University Press, 1981).

Landreth, Bill. *Out of the Inner Circle* (Bellevue, Washington: Microsoft Press, 1985).

Lobel, Jerome. *Foiling the System Breakers* (New York: McGraw-Hill, 1986).

McLean, Ephraim, and John Soden. *Strategic Planning for MIS* (New York: John Wiley and Sons, 1977).

Norman, Adrian. *Computer Insecurity* (London: Chapman and Hall, 1983).

Parker, Donn B. *Computer Security Management* (Reston, Virginia: Reston Publishing Co., 1981).

Perry, William. *Computer Control and Security* (New York: John Wiley and Sons, 1981).

————. *The Micro-Mainframe Link: The Corporate Guide to Productive Use of the Microcomputer* (New York: John Wiley and Sons, 1985).

Pfleeger, Charles. *Security in Computing* (Englewood Cliffs, New Jersey: Prentice Hall, 1989).

Rose, Michael. *Computers, Managers and Society* (Baltimore, Maryland: Penguin Books, 1969).

Synnott, William, and William Gruber. *Information Resource Management* (New York: John Wiley and Sons, 1981).

Tapscott, Don, et al. (of Trigon Systems). *Planning for Integrated Office Systems* (Homewood, Illinois: Dow Jones-Irwin, 1985).

Wiseman, Charles. *Strategy and Computers* (Homewood, Illinois: Dow Jones-Irwin, 1985).

Worthley, John A. *Managing Computers in Health Care* (Ann Arbor, Michigan: Association of University Programs in Health Administration [AUPHA] Press, 1982).

Yourdon, Edward. *Managing the System Life Cycle* (Englewood Cliffs, New Jersey: Prentice Hall, 1988).

Zuboff, Shoshana. *In the Age of the Smart Machine* (New York: Basic Books, 1988).

Computers and Education

With the advent of personal computers, there has been a rapid increase in attempts to use computers in education. In some instances, these efforts have been carefully planned and executed; in others, the machines have been placed in the home or classroom with an expectation that something would happen. The integration of computers into the instructional curriculum will be a long process.

In a general sense, all education involves the transfer of knowledge and information, but the kinds of knowledge and the learning skills required vary widely at the different stages of learning. In the first stages of education, at home and at school, children must learn basic skills and procedures while assimilating the realm of basic information. At an early age, through their explorations in movement, dance, drawing, and painting, children intuitively acquire ideas related to mathematics, logic, and abstraction. For example, the game of hopscotch teaches testing for multiple conditions, branching, and incrementing by one—all basic concepts in programming. Some educators believe that teaching children to create simple computer programs in BASIC or LOGO can provide an avenue to abstract concepts. However, most computer-aided early learning programs rely mainly on drill and repetition with an admixture of game-like graphics. The better educational programs increase the number of game-like elements but stop short of giving the kind of control found in programming.

In the later stages of primary education, the computer can be used to refine mathematical and writing skills and to introduce students to wider spheres of information. The LOGO programming language was designed to teach children geometric and programming concepts by having them write programs to control the movements of a turtle on the computer screen. As the child's social and psychological skills become more important, proficient use of computers can serve as an example of mastery of their environment. Already, some of the feats of teenage hackers suggest that creating a college-level computer environment in secondary schools might be feasible.

It is at the university level that the integration of specialized knowledge and analytic procedures with computers and information networks comes into its own. The emergence of a computer-intensive learning environment at some colleges, with the integration of personal computers, mainframes, and library resources in a campuswide network, has excited both faculty and students. Though the new information system promises to transform many elements of academic research and teaching, its marriage with the traditional curriculum is a complicated task.

At the different educational levels, there are many problems in adopting computers for learning. At primary levels, not all schools can afford to provide computers or to train staff to use them. Will the education of the underprivileged fall farther behind because of a lack of access to computers? In the high schools, will experience with computers make bright students less interested in their rote lessons? At the university level, will the computer-intensive and networked schools become an elite tier separate from the less computerized schools? Will the gap between the sciences and humanities faculties increase? Will the traditional liberal arts curriculum suffer further erosion?

Clearly, computers and information networks are becoming part of the institutions of education. As in other institutions, the new information environment will alter the management of the schools and universities. Moreover, the new modes of information storage, exchange, research, and publication are adding new elements that must be integrated with the existing instructional milieu. As before with audiovisual media, many predict a great revolution in teaching. To measure the extent of this revolution, we must look at the different levels of education in more detail.

Computers in Homes and Schools

Since 1980, many families have purchased personal computers for home office use, for games, and as a teaching aid for their children. This is particularly true of middle-class and professional households. Like the television and video games, the family computer and assorted software are usually available to the children with few limitations, such as don't get food on the computer. In the home, the computer becomes a familiar, commonplace object. It is not surrounded by the complex of rules and restrictions that are associated with computers in institutional settings.

Motivated by a desire to provide their children with computer literacy, many parents have purchased software ranging from computer-guided packages on math, grammar, and typing to programming languages such as BASIC and LOGO. Other families have user-friendly computers like the Macintosh that remove almost all obstacles to the child user. Some children have been sent to computer camp to learn programming, and others have watched their parents run word processing, spreadsheet, and graphics programs or log on to The Source or CompuServe from the home computer. In a professional household, the parents serve as models of sophisticated computer users and thus establish a role for the children to imitate. These experiences are assimilated by the children as part of their everyday environment.

What, then, is the educational impact of the computer in the home? In one respect, it becomes an extra creative space in the child's learning environment. But it does not replace any of the traditonal learning tasks the child must accomplish. Physical coordination must be acquired through active sports. The child must learn to read, write, and do arithmetic; to organize papers and reports; to speak before and listen to others; and to explicate what he has read or heard. The computer may serve as an aid in the learning of these primary skills, but in the end it is the child who must demonstate mastery to others. Only after the basic educational tasks have been accomplished can the child have a clear idea of the uses of the computer as a knowledge machine. In this sense, a computer is an advanced tool that requires a sophisticated user.

According to Roger Schank, computer scientist and psychologist, the computer has a number of strengths when used for the instruction of children:

1. Computers are fun.
2. Computers can be programmed to teach far more thoroughly and interactively than textbooks.
3. They can be individual—a child can have his own computer teacher who keeps track of progress.
4. Computers can be used by almost anyone, no matter how hyperactive or lazy.
5. Computers don't get bored or frustrated with students or with teaching. They won't punish the student or single him out for contempt.[1]

Many of the programs for computer-aided instruction rely on conventional drill and question-response methods. More innovative programs employ games, simulations, and graphics to achieve greater student involvement. One innovative program, the IBM-sponsored Writing to Read System, employs computers in conjunction with electric typwriters, a work journal, multisensory activities, a "listening" station, and a "make words" station to teach kindergarten and first-grade children to be able to write what they can say. Children learn to recognize and type words on the computer, and their learning is reinforced at the other stations. They write their own stories using phonemic spelling at the typewriters. Tested over a five-year period, this system has proven effective in teaching rudimentary reading skills.

A popular educational game, Where in the World is Carmen Sandiego? used both in schools and homes, teaches world geography and almanac use by having children play a detective on the trail of criminals. Children are provided with crimes, suspects, and clues they can identify by using the almanac provided with the game. If they guess correctly, they catch the crook. In Where in the World is Carmen Sandiego, children use the computer to make choices and navigate through the game. They cannot, however, extend or modify the game by adding facts to the game database.

Taking a different tack, Seymour Papert, an artificial intelligence researcher at Massachusetts Institute of Technology, has developed the LOGO language to teach children conceptual and programming skills. Papert and other proponents of LOGO believe that when children teach the LOGO turtle to draw geometric shapes using the recursive programming tools built into the LOGO language, they acquire at the same time an understanding of powerful mathematical and algorithmic ideas. In the LOGO environment, learning to reason is an implicit element of using turtle geometry: "LOGO challenges the children to draw a picture or solve a fun problem, and compels them to think carefully about what is going on. The kids get to do something they want to do in a logical way that ends up helping the child accomplish more than he intended. The painful and tedious task of learning a new principle in the abstract is bypassed. The child has to form the principle himself to finish a game or get through a fun situation."[2] LOGO classrooms have been set up in a number of schools, but it is too early to judge the success of LOGO in teaching powerful ideas. It is clear that children can learn to do elementary programming in LOGO and that many of them enjoy this activity.

Another perspective on programming in the early years has been developed by Sherry Turkle in *The Second Self*. Following the work of the French psychologist Jean Piaget, Turkle has focused on the role of the computer in the child's psychological development. The computer is first an evocative and puzzling object for which the child must fashion an explanation. Is it alive, is it a person, or is it a machine? In fashioning answers to this question, children also fashion different approaches to the computer. More mathematically or mechanically minded children develop a programming style that emphasizes orderly control of the machine—it does what they want. More lyrical or emotional children develop a style resting on the favor and goodwill of the computer—it may be angry or helpful. Turkle distinguishes these two approaches to the computer as the hard and soft styles of mastery.

Turkle pursues the question of styles of programming and self-images among teenage students in the secondary schools. She has found that the hard master style is preferred by hackers as evidence of their self-image of power over and control of their environment. The various aspects of the hacker culture in the secondary schools reflect the psychological needs of this transitional period between childhood and adulthood. The hard master style gives the young programmer a sense of personal worth, and the adventure of the computer games and network hacks provide obstacles and challenges to be overcome. These activities, however, if carried to an extreme, may be related to personal isolation from the teen peer group. Turkle suggests that this isolation and personal awkwardness may be a factor in the later failure of some hackers to develop a mature programming style in their college years.

We are in the early stage of educational computer use in the home and school environments. The psychological and learning effects are only beginning to become apparent. At present, in most primary and secondary schools computer use is limited to a few hours a week. Most of the student's computer time is spent on routine grammar or math drill, word processing, typing exercises, and other limited applications. In primary schools, teachers are preoccupied with basic education and there is little time to try new avenues of enrichment. Integration of computers in the basic skills curriculum has required more effort and planning than teachers had thought. Without a special effort to link computer materials with other instructional materials, the potential of computers as an educational tool has not been realized.

Educators can imagine a multimedia classroom of the future enriched by computers, televison, and electronic musical instruments, with optical discs for mass storage of texts, music, and images and with network links to information databases. Only a few experimental multimedia classrooms exist, but all the technical elements to create them are available. In the future, if the funds are available, schools and universities may provide such an integrated media environment for teaching.

Computers and Learning in the University Environment

University engineers and scientists designed the first computers. They improved the early machines and developed the methods to program them. University research laboratories were among the first major users of the machines. The initial applications were for the laborious numerical computations associated with research in the physical sciences, and computers remained largely the province of the hard sciences for a number of years. Other early computer users were social scientists working with statistical interpretation of census and survey data. Computing services were usually provided through a centralized computing center. Data and programs were stored on IBM cards and card readers were used for data input. Batch mode processing with 24-hour turnaround time was commonplace into the 1970s.

A campus computing network was established at Dartmouth College in the 1960s and was a forerunner of the networks developed at many universities in the 1970s. These networks provided interactive computer access to some of the faculty and students. Campus networks were usually composed of a central mainframe, terminals, card readers, and printers. Minicomputers were also associated with the networks at larger universities. Access to the network through terminals was often a privilege restricted to advanced computer users, and most other users continued to have only batch mode privileges. In 1973, the campus computing centers in the University of California system used the following machines:

Berkeley—Four Nova 1200s, one CDC 6400, one Micro 810, two Novas, and two PDP-8s

Davis—One Burroughs 6700, one Decision, and one Nova 1200

Irvine—One PDP-10, one Sigma 7, one Omnus 1, and one PDP-8

Los Angeles—One IBM 360/91

Riverside—One IBM 360/50

San Diego—One Burroughs 6700, two CDC 160s, one CDC 1700, one CDC 3600, one IBM 360/20, and five Micro 800s

San Francisco—One IBM 360/50 and one HP 2115A

Santa Barbara—One IBM 360/75 and one IBM 360/20

Santa Cruz—One IBM 360/40 and two PDP 11s[3]

Outside of the computing centers, a number of small machines were used in the larger research laboratories for data collection and scientific calculations. University administrative data processing was carried out on an IBM 360/30 and an IBM 360/65 at Berkeley and on an IBM 360/30 and an IBM 360/40 at Los Angeles. On the whole, university computing resources were limited in comparison with government and business data processing systems of the period.

The relatively stable pattern of computer use in the 1970s gave way to a dramatically changing situation in the 1980s with the introduction of personal computers. The placement of networked computers and terminals in student workrooms, libraries, administrative, and faculty offices has extended computer use throughout the universities. The demand for new hardware and software and courses for student and staff computer users has overwhelmed the computer centers and computer science departments.

At a few universities, all students are provided with or required to have personal computers. At other schools, the number of terminals on campus was expanded and large purchases of personal computers were made. The computer intensive environment that developed at these schools was often vital and exciting. Students became involved in programming; word processing; some use of computer-aided instruction; and various statistical, simulation, and experimental class projects. Departments in the physical and social sciences were able to set up personal computer workrooms for their students, and this, in turn, has spurred the increasing undergraduate use of statistical and mathematical techniques formerly restricted to graduate students. Departments of engineering, architecture, and graphic design have set up personal computer design labs where students can use the available graphics packages for their design projects.

Before the introduction of microcomputers, many scientists had to write their own programs for the mainframe. This limited the use of computers in research and instruction. The proliferation of scientific and engineering software has now made it easier to work with the computer than without it. For scientific laboratory research, engineering testing, and statistical analysis, a large number of analytic software packages have been developed or ported to the personal computer from existing mainframe software. Scientific packages provide for data acquisition, signal processing, and process control monitoring. Analog to digital converters take signals from laboratory equipment and translate the data to personal computers. Laboratory notebook and data record software help the researcher to track experiments. Specialized software has been written for circuit design, thermal analysis, frequency spectrum analysis, and mechanical testing. Mathematical and statistical packages can be used to solve equations and to analyze, graph, or plot data. Scientific word processors that provide support for mathematical formulas, tables, and graphs have been created for the preparation of technical reports. These software tools are available for both student and faculty research and provide much greater flexibility in laboratory work than existed before.

Starting with personal computers, non-science faculty also have become involved with the mainframe and computer workroom resources on their campuses. An interesting example of the computer's potential to assist instruction in the humanities is the Writer's Workbench, which is part of the UNIX system. Writer's Workbench was designed to analyze prose texts for punctuation, spelling, style, and usage. The style analysis program, for example, can indentify passive constructions, grammatical mistakes, awkward phrases, and other problems. These are reported to the author, who can then make appropriate changes. Programs modeled on the Writer's Workbench could be used in the many English composition classes to show students the commonplace errors in their writing. However, to do this, students must enter their papers on the campus computer network so that style and usage can be analyzed. On their own computers, students can use the grammar and spelling checkers that have been developed as adjuncts to word processing programs.

Beyond scientific analysis, graphics, and word processing, computers offer the faculty a variety of specialized applications for their subject areas. Alongside existing software, faculty can create instructional programs with authoring tools to demonstrate various topics in the classroom. The Academic Courseware Exchange established by Kinko's Service Corporation promotes the movement of faculty-authored software between universities. The Courseware Exchange sells authoring tools to faculty for writing instructional software and sells the resulting packages for a small fee. The current Courseware Exchange catalog has programs in nineteen different disciplines, with applications as varied as a molecular editor, a transmission line simulator, a logic tutor, a prose instructor, torts exercises, and an eighteenth-century historical simulation.

As part of its program for computers in education, Apple Computer supports the publication of *Wheels for the Mind* by Boston College. This journal describes new instructional programs using computers and new software at different universities. Another program for development and exchange of instructional software for academic workstations is being promoted by EDUCOM in conjunction with Carnegie-Mellon University. With Carnegie-Mellon, nineteen universities have formed an Inter-University Educational Computing Consortium. Development is underway on a software authoring system (Andrew) and on a proposed academic workstation with a UNIX operating environment. At present, consortium members are writing instructional software on Macintosh and IBM personal computers and SUN workstations.

Efforts are also being made to design "intelligent tutor" programs that will use artificial intelligence techniques for instruction. Relying on an expert diagnostic system, the intelligent tutor can analyze the student's errors and misconceptions and restructure the learning tasks to work toward correction of the mistakes. The logical and psychological model of learning embedded in the intelligent tutor breaks with the linear, step-by-step progression embedded in most programmed instruction. Although brilliant students may learn through the processes of intuition and insight, most students could overcome commonplace errors with an intelligent tutor. Advances in artificial intelligence research are also producing an interesting convergence of psychological models of human learning and computational models of machine learning that may eventually contribute to changes in the instruction of both humans and machines.

The spread of computing and computer use in the universities is not without some problems. Although many faculty and students have become involved with the new machines and software, many others have not. Besides the cost of a personal computer, a number of barriers have created problems for the novice. The mainframe-oriented computer center environment is often intimidating for both faculty and students. Some of the same problems found between data processing departments and their organizations exist between campus computer centers and their users. The computer center staff were accustomed to dealing with science students already familiar with computers and were not prepared for the upsurge of demands from humanities and social science students. Hardware incompatibilities frustrated efforts to link departmental computers with campus mainframes. The general interest in computer literacy and rapid increase in the number of computer science majors placed a strain on the teaching resources of the computer science departments.

Several avenues have been found around these barriers. Separate computer workrooms have been set up for students in the social sciences, humanities, and arts. Computer center staff have revised and expanded user information materials, and computer training courses are run for faculty and staff to encourage user self-sufficiency and decrease reliance on the center. New computer installations are planned with hardware compatibility in mind. However, many of these solutions are only temporary. As the faculty and students become more sophisticated, their demands and questions increase. Computer center staff cannot respond to all requests. Lacking the resources, the universities may not develop the computer-intensive environment that users can imagine.

Information Gateways

As the university computing environment changes, a new perception of the library and computer center as information gateways is emerging. The automation of the library, with online catalogs and linkages to various database vendors (such as Dialog, BRS, and Orbit), is changing the pattern of library use. Previously a storehouse of books, journals, and documents, the library is becoming a gateway to these resources stored in electronic form. The use of CD-ROM discs and players to distribute different periodical indices and databases is only beginning. As printing costs continue to rise and electronic storage costs fall, the transition to electronic media will accelerate.

There are advantages and disadvantages to this change. On one hand, it is possible to search the library catalog from a terminal on campus or a personal computer at home. A topic search can be ordered on one of the database services. Libraries are saving money and storage space by decreasing their subscriptions to periodicals and journals. Hard copy of an article can be obtained from the database service after a search is completed. In the future, journals may move to electronic publication, with hard copy only being provided on request. Using automated search programs, researchers can establish a profile of research interests and a search schedule, and thereby new material of interest in the literature will be reported to the researchers when it appears.

On the negative side, some of the advantages of browsing in a library stack area or through a journal are lost in the electronic environment. We often read articles in a journal that we did not initially seek out, or a book on the shelf may catch our eye. These serendipitous effects are changed in an electronic search. Because we may not have drawn the search parameters correctly, we have to sift through a variety of title-related but substantively unrelated material. In this case, serendipity does not have the positive side effects it does when browsing in the stacks or in a journal. To offset this loss, a selection of books and articles across the disciplines that are considered noteworthy or interesting could be posted on the library network. In this way, we can partly restore the potential for browsing across specialized subjects and disciplines. As database search programs are given some artificial intelligence capabilities, it may be possible for the program to learn a person's areas of interest and retrieve all relevant materials. The knowledge demon, acting autonomously once set up, would go through information networks seeking citations and materials and then present these materials to the researcher on the computer.

At present, database searches in the physical and biological sciences may be more effective than in the social sciences, where intellectual movements and terminology are more varied:

> When we compare the topic definitions and classifications in the humanities with those in the natural and biological sciences, we are struck by how ahistorical, or "progressive" the latter are. . . . there is a much narrower temporal span of "active" literature for researchers to know. In areas of theory and experimentation, one finds a relatively rigid vocabulary and classification system. These qualities favor accuracy and completeness of scientific reference work.
>
> In the humanities and social sciences, on the other hand, the researcher is confronted with "movements" that are often mutually indifferent to one another. In political science, Marxists and behaviorists make no attempt to achieve a common vocabulary.[4]

In order to improve the efficiency of searches in the social sciences and humanities, an effort to regularize the terminology or track intellectual movements is needed.

As with the library, the growing number of network connections made through the computer center have made it an information gateway. Alongside regular computing tasks and local electronic mail, the computer center serves as the link to inter-university networks such as Bitnet, Arpanet, and the UNIX network. These networks connect university computers and their users across the country and overseas. To handle the increasing flow of data through the existing inter-university networks, efforts are underway in the U.S. Congress to fund the building of a high-capacity, backbone computer network to link regional scientific networks.

Through terminals or personal computers, the faculty have access to the computer center and to inter-university networks. University administrative memoranda and communications from colleagues and students can reach faculty through this channel. With the increasing electronic exchanges of research information and the high cost of book and journal production, electronic publication on the networks may become part of scholarly research. Recently, some conferences on the UNIX network have adopted a refereed system similar to that used by the editorial boards of printed journals. This system controls the quality of information presented to the conference. As the electronic exchange of research information and findings matures, other modes of quality control will emerge.

New Models, New Metaphors, and New Methods

Alongside their routine use by students and faculty, computers are triggering other changes in the university. In the long run, a significant impact arises from changes in the models, metaphors, and methods used in research and teaching. From the 1950s on, scientists involved with computer programming have drawn an analogy between human problem solving and computer algorithms. For each successive model of artificial intelligence, language translation, or computer spatial representation, a corresponding model of human reasoning, language, and perception has been proposed. Analyses of computer information processing have been accompanied by analyses of human thought processes, and the field of cognitive science has flourished as a result.

Before the extensive use of personal computers and minicomputers in the universities, the exploration of computer modeling and information processing was limited to small specialist circles. As use has expanded, thinking about and with computers has moved into nonspecialist circles. Talk about computers, both hardware and software, has become commonplace around the faculty center and the student union. A new set of terms and metaphors derived from computers and programming has passed into everyday academic parlance.

Over time, the popularization of computers may lead to a significant theoretical and methodological shift in thought. As researchers strive to use the computer in their studies, several changes can occur. The problem under investigation can be restructured to make it computable; in the process, the problem comes to be seen in a new perspective. With problems that cannot be restructured, the investigator is forced to develop new methods of classification and analysis to make the subject fit the machine. In computational terms, discrete finite problems are preferable. Researchers must either decompose their subjects into pieces that can be analysed or discover new models to represent the subject.

In *Turing's Man,* a philosophical discussion of the computational universe, David Bolter contrasts the logics of infinity and finitude. The computer embodies a finite logic and mathematics. The transfinite and the undecidable are beyond the bounds of the computer. Yet, as the computer emerges as a defining technology, topics that cannot be computed may fall out of favor. There is a curious quandary in this situation. Despite the speed and memory of the computer, it is inherently limited to the analysis of finite problems. In astronomy and astrophysics, the computer in concert with telescopes allows the perception and measurement of ever farther reaches of the universe. But the research problems framed by astronomers and astrophysicists—of galactic origins and the death of stars—reflect the realm in which the human mind seeks answers. Without computer coordination, the multiple-mirror telescope in Arizona could not function. The alignment of the mirrors and the recording and analysis of the data rely on computers; but the questions of galactic cosmology are beyond the scope of any existing computer.

Modeling, Simulation, and Graphics

In the sciences and humanities, computers stimulate the use of methods for statistical analysis and graphic representation of data. Modeling and simulation have developed in several different directions. These include

1. Construction of models and simulations that students could manipulate to understand the static and dynamic states of particular systems (e.g., the workings of a power plant, the heart and the circulatory system, the courts and a criminal case docket, or public voting patterns and legislative actions).
2. Construction of models and simulations to display patterns of disorder or dysfunction on which students could practice alternative methods of correction, repair, or treatment.
3. Simulations of decision-making situations using rule-based inference and expert systems. Students are guided through the decision process and learn the rules relating a set of conditions to a probable outcome (e.g., rules relating symptoms, diagnosis, and treatment).[5]

The models and simulations range from single cases to complex systems. Smaller models can be run on personal computers, but the more complex systems require the resources of a mainframe or supercomputer.

To make the power of supercomputers available to more research scientists, since 1985 the National Science Foundation has supported five regional supercomputer centers at Cornell University, University of California–San Diego, Princeton University, University of Illinois–Champaign/Urbana, and a joint University of Pittsburgh/Carnegie-Mellon University center. These centers make their supercomputers available through networks to researchers throughout the country. The San Diego Supercomputer Center, for example, is affiliated with more than twenty universities and research institutions in the western region of the country. The centers provide training seminars on supercomputer use to increase the number of researchers familiar with the machines. Time on the machines is allocated to selected projects put forward by proposals from center affiliates.

These supercomputers have been used primarily for problems that involve the assembly, modeling, and analysis of very large data sets such as those generated in subatomic particle research, modeling of molecules and molecular interactions, fluid dynamics, weather modeling, observations from radio telescopes and construction of galaxy models, medical imaging, and modeling of economic systems. With a supercomputer, the models can be as complex as is required and the time needed to analyze the data sets does not run into several days, as it would on most mainframe systems. Models or simulations can be displayed through scientific visualization. With specialized graphics, dynamic phenomena can be visualized using surface or volume rendering, false color assignment, opacity and density variation, and shading techniques. Scientific visualization reveals previously unseen details in the dynamic interactions under examination. As researchers with complex problems and large data sets become familiar with remote access to supercomputers, new research projects will be developed to exploit the power of these machines.

More models and simulations will be developed and used in instruction when graphics workstations become widely available to faculty and students. Already, as capabilities increase and costs decrease, graphics workstations, plotters, and drafting software are changing the curriculum in engineering, architecture, and design. Workstations have become the standard environment for technical design in industry, and students in the technical disciplines must become familiar with them. Students in engineering and architecture are learning electronic drafting and sketching. With computer-assisted drafting (CAD) graphics software to manipulate two- and three-dimensional models, the student can view and modify different design solutions. Instructors in design have long recognized the advantages of graphic models, but before the availability of graphics workstations the preparation of numerous drawings and models was time consuming. The workstation and graphics software have decreased the time needed from conception to model.

The full implications of using extensive graphic representations in instruction are far-reaching. Many concepts and relationships in the sciences, mathematics, and the social sciences are suited to presentation with charts, graphs, maps, and models. Mathematicians, for example, can represent equations in both algebraic notation and graphic form. The graphic presentation reinforces and clarifies the linear notation. In geography and geology, mapping software for workstations has facilitated the preparation of high-quality maps and charts. As instructors and students become more familiar with graphic presentation of their material, the graphic modes of thought will attain greater equality with linear modes of expression.

In physics and applied mathematics, new research areas have been opened using the computer to graphically display and record previously unseen and unanalyzed phenomena. Chaotic phenomena, like turbulent flows and storms, have been simulated on the computer, and areas of stability within turbulence have been discovered. Before graphics simulation, the visualization and detailed analysis of the dynamic systems found in chaotic phenomena had been very difficult. In mathematics, simulation has advanced the study of topological surfaces and the new set of fractals is being charted and explored. With computer graphics, mathematicians can observe changes in mathematical objects in multidimensional spaces and then construct the formal mathematics for what they have observed. Computer programming itself has lead to studies of efficient algorithms, recursion, and symmetry.

For the social sciences, the inter-university networks and statistical data banks create an environment in which data sharing and secondary statistical analysis are feasible. With graphics workstations, statistical and demographic data can be converted to maps and charts for wider dissemination of social scientific information. Documentary and pictorial materials are also becoming more widely available through the use of CD-ROM discs. CD-ROM discs holding statistical data, graphics, maps, or pictorial information are useful both for research and classroom purposes. We can anticipate that in the near future students will be acquainted with the available information resources (CD-ROM, data banks, and networks) in secondary schools. College-level courses will then, appropriately, be concerned with techniques of data collection, analysis, presentation, and modeling.

Information Retrieval and Hypertext

The arrangement and retrieval of information stored in computers and data banks has raised unprecedented organizational questions. Viewing, arranging, and retrieving research materials placed on a tabletop is a fairly simple matter. Arranging and retrieving files from a filing cabinet is also fairly straightforward and doing so from a room of filing cabinets only somewhat less so. But arranging and retrieving files from several rooms of filing cabinets is another matter. This last situation is analogous to what we face with electronic data banks and CD-ROM.

Libraries have dealt with the electronic cataloging problem for printed materials by adopting a standard catalog format based on the Library of Congress system. The Online Computer Library Center (OCLC) serves as a coordinator and clearinghouse for member libraries as they make the transition to computerized library systems. Government and business organizations have created standard record formats for their database systems. A new discipline, information science, has been created to study the most efficient modes of information storage and retrieval. Scientific information and knowledge can use these forms of database storage but also require less structured and more syncretic formats for information storage and retrieval.

Recognizing the need for new electronic ways to structure knowledge and scientific information, researchers are using hypertext software to make new relationship patterns within and between areas of knowledge. Working from Douglas Englebart's knowledge, augmentation research at Stanford, and Ted Nelson's hypertext concepts, software engineers have created tools to connect and reference electronic texts and images in new and unusual ways. Bill Atkinson's HyperCard program, packaged with the Macintosh computer, provides a stack of electronic cards that can be written on, arranged, and linked to store information. Unlike paper cards, which are physically sorted into different piles to rearrange the information, HyperCard screens can be electronically linked to each other in several different ways. Thus, several different search paths are possible when moving through the electronic stack.

HyperCard and other hypertext programs allow researchers to create nodes or buttons within a text that refer to related materials, which in turn may link to others, in an open structure. Points on a city map, for example, can be linked to landmark descriptions, pictures, and more detailed maps. These in turn may be linked to other pertinent information. The user can move forward, backward, or jump around within the hypertext structure. Beyond a simple stack, an index or overview of the hypertext structure is required to provide orientation for the user. Although the entire hypertext document cannot be presented as a linear document like a book, it can be accessed and explored through the computer and associated media. Because hypertext allows the reader to find a personalized path into the subject matter, researchers anticipate that hypertext documents will be a useful and interesting way to introduce students to new subjects. Hypertext links and overviews will also serve as a way of organizing and accessing the large amounts of information stored in CD-ROM systems.

In combination with CD-ROM, hypertext programs can become the center for multimedia presentations using textual materials, graphs, pictures, or sound. The instructional potential of computers and CD-ROM in both the universities and high schools is great. As computer use develops in the universities, some programs will serve as models for similar programs in high schools. The high school science program is one area where personal computers can be readily integrated with instruction. Integration of computers and CD-ROM in other high school instructional areas will take more effort. In time, teachers and students will have ready access to computers, data banks, and analytical tools to address in innovative ways the issues and problems raised in their discussions. In the information-rich environment of computer-aided instruction and multimedia presentations, the role of teachers as mentors and guides to their students will become more critical.

Notes

1. Roger C. Schank, *The Cognitive Computer* (Reading, Massachusetts: Addison-Wesley, 1984), p. 204.

2. *Ibid.,* p. 206.

3. Ephraim McLean and John Soden, *Strategic Planning for MIS* (New York: John Wiley and Sons, 1977), pp. 330–331.

4. John S. Lawrence, *The Electronic Scholar* (Norwood, New Jersey: Ablex Publishing, 1984), p. 107.

5. See D. Ingram and C. J. Dickinson, "A Review of Modelling and Simulation Techniques in Medical Education," in Ewart R. Carson and Derek G. Cramp, eds., *Computers and Control in Clinical Medicine* (New York: Plenum Press, 1985).

Selected Bibliography

Ambron, Sueann, and Kristina Hooper. *Interactive Multimedia* (Redmond, Washington: Microsoft Press, 1988).

Barrett, Edward, ed. *The Society of Text* (Cambridge, Massachusetts: The MIT Press, 1989).

Bolter, J. David. *Turing's Man* (Chapel Hill: University of North Carolina Press, 1984).

Campbell, Patricia, and Greta Fein, eds. *Young Children and Microcomputers* (Englewood Cliffs, New Jersey: Prentice Hall, 1986).

Chen, Milton, and William Paisley, eds. *Children and Microcomputers* (Beverly Hills, California: Sage Publications, 1985).

Coats, Robert B., and Andrew Parkin. *Computer Models in the Social Sciences* (Cambridge, Massachusetts: Winthrop Publishers, 1977).

Gleick, James. *Chaos* (New York: Viking Penguin, 1987).

Goldmann, Nahum. *Online Research and Retrieval with Microcomputers* (Blue Ridge Summit, Pennsylvania: Tab Books, 1985).

Ingram, D., and C. J. Dickinson. "A Review of Modelling and Simulation Techniques in Medical Education." In Ewart R. Carson and Derek G. Cramp, eds. *Computers and Control in Clinical Medicine* (New York: Plenum Press, 1985).

Karin, Sidney, and Norris Smith. *The Supercomputer Era* (Boston, Massachusetts: Harcourt Brace Jovanovich, 1987).

Kearsley, Greg. *Artificial Intelligence and Instruction* (Reading, Massachusetts: Addison-Wesley, 1987).

Kim, Scott. *Inversions* (Peterborough, New Hampshire: Byte Books, 1981).

Klein, Elisa L. *Children and Computers* (San Francisco, California: Jossey-Bass, 1985).

Lambert, Steve, and Suzanne Ropiequet, eds. *CD ROM* (Redmond, Washington: Microsoft Press, 1986).

Lawrence, John S. *The Electronic Scholar* (Norwood, New Jersey: Ablex Publishing, 1984).

McLean, Ephraim, and John Soden. *Strategic Planning for MIS* (New York: John Wiley and Sons, 1977).

Martin, John Henry, and Ardy Friedberg. *Writing to Read* (New York: Warner Books, 1986).

Michie, Donald, and Rory Johnson. *The Knowledge Machine* (New York: William Morrow and Company, 1985).

Nelson, Theodor. *Computer Lib* (South Bend, Indiana: The Distributors, 1974).

Pagels, Heinz R. *The Dreams of Reason* (New York: Simon & Schuster, 1988).

Papert, Seymour. *Mindstorms* (New York: Basic Books, 1980).

Pea, Roy D., and Karen Sheingold. *Mirrors of Minds* (Norwood, New Jersey: Ablex Publishing, 1987).

Peterson, Ivars. *The Mathematical Tourist* (New York: W. H. Freeman and Co., 1988).

Provenzo, Eugene F. *Beyond the Gutenberg Galaxy* (New York: Teachers College Press, 1986).

Roszak, Theodore. *The Cult of Information* (New York: Pantheon Books, 1986).

Schank, Roger C., with Peter Childers. *The Cognitive Computer* (Reading, Massachusetts: Addison-Wesley, 1984).

Schank, Roger C., and Kenneth Colby, eds. *Computer Models of Thought and Language* (San Francisco, California: W. H. Freeman and Co., 1973).

Sloan, Douglas, ed. *The Computer in Education* (New York: Teachers College Press, 1985).

Sussman, Marvin B., ed. *Personal Computers and the Family* (New York: Haworth Press, 1985).

Turkle, Sherry. *The Second Self* (New York: Simon & Schuster, 1984).

Computers, Politics, and Government

The computer has, since its inception, played a role in government and politics in our society. The military funded the development of the first electronic computer during World War II, and military defense systems and government record management systems were among the initial large-scale applications. The federal government, through the various agencies that collect national and international data, remains one of the major institutional users of computers. Though political leaders initially conceived of computers as large calculators or electronic filing cabinets, they now recognize that computers are changing the nature of government itself. It is this change we must try to assess.

In certain respects, computerization in government has the same impacts that can be found in other organizations. The transition from paper to electronic media for the preparation and storage of documents and records follows a similar pattern. The unique aspects of governmental computer usage emerge with the special legal requirements and limitations that we place on our government. Several questions have been raised about the government's use of computers:

1. What is the proper extent of government data-gathering activities?
2. Should the records of government agencies be centralized?
3. What access should individuals have to government records?
4. How are customary and legal conceptions of privacy changed by government and private data-gathering activities?

5. When do electronic records become legal documents that must be retained?

These questions have been the focus of a wide-ranging debate in Congress and the media, and a number of legislative acts have been passed to regulate data gathering by government and commercial agencies.

The institutional effects of computers in government are far-reaching, giving rise to what David Burnham has called "the computer state." Along with the threat to privacy, computers are changing party politics and the democratic process, government and military planning, and the processes of law enforcement. The potential for increased centralization of government information and increased intervention in the everyday life of society already exists. In a totalitarian state, without democratic restraints on goverment, computers could facilitate surveillance and control of both dissidents and the population in general. In a democratic society, we must consider the degree to which the benign powers of the computer state might be turned to surveillance or political intimidation.

The Public Image of Computers

The political tradition of our society has placed considerable emphasis on the twin notions of liberty and privacy as the bases for democratic politics and a society free from undue government intrusion. The emergence of an increasingly organized institutional world in this century, culminating with the computerization of organizations, has shifted the setting in which we attempt to use our rights to liberty and privacy. To some, perhaps, these rights may seem out of date. To most of us, however, they are crucial elements in the limitation of institutional power and arbitrariness.

The public image of computers in politics has not remained constant over the last decades. In the 1950s, computers in government and politics were treated as a wonderful novelty. In 1952, on the night of the presidential election, a UNIVAC 1 was used by CBS to predict the outcome of the vote. The engineers at Remington-Rand had programmed the computer to analyze the returns in relation to voting patterns in the preceding two elections. Early in the evening, the UNIVAC predicted a landslide for Eisenhower. As this was not expected by the CBS analysts or by the engineers, it was not reported over the air. Instead, the UNIVAC program was altered to make the prediction fit the political expectations. Later, when the Eisenhower trend in the vote was definite, CBS reported UNIVAC's initial prediction with an explanation from

Arthur Draper, Remington-Rand's research director: "Well, we had a lot of troubles tonight. Strangely enough, they were all human and not the machine. When UNIVAC made its first prediction, we just didn't believe it. So we asked UNIVAC to forget a lot of trend information, assuming it was wrong. . . . [But] as more votes came in, the odds came back, and it is now evident that we should have had nerve enough to believe the machine in the first place."[1] In election forecasting, the computer passed quickly from novelty item to standard element in the election broadcast. Political poll results analyzed by computer have become a standard part of political reporting and election campaign planning.

In government settings, the initial novelty of the computer was displayed with demonstrations of its speed in handling records. This soon gave way to the routine world of IBM cards and computer snafus. A new image of computers emerged in the political controversies of the 1960s, when the IBM card was used by demonstrators as a symbol of their frustration with institutional aloofness. The caution "Do not fold, spindle or mutilate" printed on each IBM card became a political slogan denoting institutional preference for categorical data and insensitivity to human needs and weaknesses. Government computers were cast in the role of enemy or tyrant; many people felt reduced to the status of IBM numbers. Some political activists began to suspect that government computers were being used to keep files on those who exercised the right to dissent. Later revelations during the Watergate affair of FBI wiretap activities, executive branch misuse of IRS information, domestic covert operations, CIA use of the National Student Association for domestic spying, and military surveillance of antiwar activists show that these suspicions were not without justification.

The Issue of Privacy

By the mid-1960s, public discussion of government computers began to focus on the issues of privacy, government data banks, and electronic surveillance. The publication of Alan Westin's *Privacy and Freedom* in 1967 and Arthur R. Miller's *The Assault on Privacy* in 1971 set the stage for a series of legislative hearings, studies, and enactments. The laws that emerged from the privacy debate were influenced by the recommendations in Westin's book and sought to "redress the balance" that the computer, electronic eavesdropping, and other innovations in surveillance technology had disturbed.

In *Privacy and Freedom,* Alan Westin examined the growing institutional collection and use of personal information. The electronic data bank plays a central role in the organization, retrieval, and dissemination of personal information required by institutions for legal or bureaucratic reasons. Advances in electronic technology have greatly facilitated the practices of physical, psychological, and data surveillance. Recognizing these new capabilities, Westin raised several issues:

1. Is the information collected necessary to the functioning of the institution or could alternatives be found?
2. Is the information accurate and timely?
3. Are people aware the information is being collected and do they consent?
4. Can the institutions protect the privacy and confidentiality of the information?
5. Can people examine and amend their files?

Westin recommended several procedural and legal reforms to address these issues, including measures to ensure the accuracy of the data collected, to limit the transfer of personal information between government agencies, and to allow individuals access to their files. These recommendations were included in the formulation of the Fair Credit Reporting Act of 1970 and the Privacy Act of 1974.

Although the federal legislation of 1970 and 1974 extended the legal framework of protections for individual privacy, it also legitimated the increasing data-gathering activities of public and private institutions. In a 1973 book, *Private Lives and Public Surveillance,* James Rule critically questioned the functional necessity and social cost of the increasing surveillance of the public. To understand public surveillance and data-gathering systems, Rule carried out studies of police surveillance, vehicle and driver licensing, and national health insurance in Britain, and of consumer credit reporting and the BankAmericard system in the United States. Through these case studies he was able to explore the institutional conditions that create a desire or need to make fine-grained discriminations among people in a large and anonymous clientele. For example, in order to control the misuse of credit cards, retail stores electronically check an individual's credit balance to obtain approval for credit card purchases. For loans and other financial transactions, credit-reporting services that provide fine-grained customer information have become a major online business. From an institutional point of view, this may seem reasonable. But, Rule suggests, the loss in privacy entailed by the routine credit check should be weighed against the institutional cost of credit fraud. Is the loss in privacy from ongoing financial surveillance offset by the gain in limiting credit card abuse? Rule and others feel that the steady erosion of personal and financial privacy is a much greater loss.

In his analysis, Rule found that several factors are increasing the size of surveillance systems: 1) growth in the amount of useful data kept per client; 2) increasing subtlety in using the data; 3) growing centralization of files; 4) growing speed of information flow; 5) increased effectiveness of contact between system and client; and 6) improved procedures for client identification and linkage to files.[2] The increased capacity of the systems makes it easier to discriminate among individuals and identify those who deviate from accepted norms or are otherwise undesirable, minimizing the risks from such things as bad checks or credit card fraud. But the systems are costly to maintain and operate. Rule argues that the growing loss of privacy is a greater risk to individual liberty than the cost to the institutions of forgoing additional credit information. Whether we agree with Rule's position or not, we should understand that few limits have been placed on the continued growth and use of public and private surveillance systems.

Federal Data Banks

Since the economic depression of the 1930s, the operations of federal agencies have been extended to monitor, regulate, and provide benefits to almost all sectors of our society. In order to achieve these objectives, government agencies keep files on most citizens, organizations, and institutions. Under the provisions of the Privacy Act of 1974, 97 agencies reported the existence of 6,753 systems of records with more than 3.85 billion individual records (these do not include the secret records of the intelligence agencies).[3] The major federal agencies collecting personal data and statistics include the Bureau of the Census, the National Center for Health Statistics, the Bureau of Labor Statistics, the Social Security Administration, the Internal Revenue Service (IRS), and the Federal Bureau of Investigation (FBI). The Office of Research and Statistics of the Social Security Administration, for example, reported the existence of fifty-five systems of records. Several of the agencies release anonymous data sets (census data, health surveys) for public use and analysis. The FBI operates the National Crime Information Center (NCIC), which is linked to state and local law enforcement agencies. On a nationwide basis, NCIC maintains files containing the criminal histories of offenders, their current status, and their whereabouts.

The computerization of federal record systems has increased the potential for the centralization of government information. In 1966, a proposal for a National Statistical Data Center was placed before Congress. After a series of controversial hearings in which fears of government snooping and threats to privacy were raised, the idea was abandoned. The Privacy Act of 1974 placed limits on the tendency toward centralization by restricting to "routine uses" the information collected by agencies. The act also placed limits on the interagency exchange of personal data. Because agencies are now more sensitive to confidentiality of their files, they have become more careful in disseminating their files and data. Within an agency, personal information used for routine purposes can circulate. Only anonymous information is sent to other agencies. However, shifts in government policy can change the interpretation of the Privacy Act. For example, the Reagan administration matched lists of federal employees with lists of welfare recipients to check for welfare fraud. The courts have upheld the government's actions in this matching program.

Beyond the administrative and investigative data banks held by the government exists another tier of data systems operated by the intelligence and defense agencies. These include the data banks of the Central Intelligence Agency (CIA), the National Security Agency (NSA), the Defense Department, and the Secret Service. Documents revealed during the Watergate period established that intelligence agencies had been involved in domestic surveillance and covert operations. The intelligence community has argued before Congress that these revelations damaged the operations of the intelligence agencies. In subsequent efforts to restore intelligence-gathering capacity, public information about these agencies has again been restricted. Even congressional oversight committees have difficulty monitoring the activities of the CIA and NSA. It is known that the NSA eavesdrops on overseas communications networks, but to what extent this activity carries over into the domestic network is unclear. Because foreign intelligence agencies also carry out surveillance of international communications, we can assume a general absence of privacy in the international networks.

Government Organization and Information Systems

Privacy issues are a central concern in the government use of computers, but computers also change the way the government operates, the services delivered, and the political system itself. One change is increasing coordination between different parts of the government and between federal, state, and local authorities. This has been particularly true in the law enforcement arena, where computer networks are moving criminal records between different police authorities. The design of the law enforcement information system serves as a model for other government agencies. For agencies cooperating in an information network, whether in welfare or taxation, there are several important institutional effects:

1. Standardization of record and file formats
2. Rapid sharing of information between government levels
3. Establishment of statewide and nationwide databases
4. Increased accountability between levels of the system
5. Rapid movement of information to point of contact with the respective clientele

The increased efficiency of government agencies that these information systems provide has both positive and negative aspects. From an administrative point of view, the system is more rational and effective. But from the client's point of view, it may be too rational and effective. A taxpayer undergoing an IRS tax audit may find his shoebox records file is no match for the agency's computers. A welfare mother may not be able to argue against the detailed regulations and case record used by the case worker to process her claim. In both cases, the information in the agency computer system gives the administrator an advantage when dealing with the client.

Among federal agencies, the Department of Defense (DOD) leads in establishing standards for information systems used by the government. The Defense Department has been a major sponsor of computer and artificial intelligence research, promoted the design and use of the programming language ADA, and is developing a computer-aided logistics support system to standardize data and communications among all DOD computers. Other federal agencies may later use these standards to link their computers.

As federal agencies have extended their use of computers a government computing community has developed. A biweekly newspaper, *Government Computer News*, provides information on changes in government computer policy, new developments in the different agencies, and a forum for advertisers who wish to reach government computer users. Several computer conferences are held in Washington, D.C., each year. Both the Federal Computer Conference and the Government Computer Expo, for example, provide a variety of seminars, speeches, and workshops and a product exposition. Both conferences draw support from computer professionals in government agencies and the private sector.

Strategic Planning, Battle Management, and the Automation of War

In various government agencies, computers are used to develop budget forecasts, track projects, and run what-if simulations. In the defense area, strategic and war-game simulations are an essential element of military strategy and training. As government agencies use computers more, computer forecasts, plans, and simulations become a set part of the decison-making process. In many areas, these forecasts and simulations are mundane and innocuous. In the military, strategic, and foreign policy areas of decision making, the potential consequences of computer assistance are more serious.

Over the last two decades, the playing out of strategic and war-game scenarios has become an established part of the national security system. These simulations are used by strategic and military planners to consider alternative courses of action in hypothetical crisis situations. However, as is often the case with simulations of political situations, the war game cannot anticipate all of the elements found in a real crisis situation but only those built into the simulation. As the politicians and military leaders become accustomed to the world of simulations, there is a danger they will confuse it with the more complex real world. Courses of action that work in a simulation may prove disastrous in the real world. The jargon and thought of government and military planners has absorbed many terms from the world of simulations. To the public audience, these terms obscure more than they clarify the process of government and military planning.

Over the years, substantial funds for research and pilot projects in computer science have been provided by the Department of Defense, and practical applications derived from the research have become part of the strategic defense system. Since the microcomputer became a practical reality, all branches of the military have moved rapidly to modernize computer systems in all parts of the military structure. In 1988, out of a $16.8 billion federal budget for information technology, the Department of Defense share was $7.65 billion. This compares with $1.6 billion for the Department of Health and Human Services, $1.2 billion for the Treasury Department, $1.1 billion for NASA, $624 million for the Agriculture Department, and less for other federal agencies. The military and intelligence agencies easily take the largest share of federal government spending for information technology.

In the last decade, the military has developed and deployed a new generation of microprocessor-enhanced "smart" weapons. These programmable weapons are part of an integrated battle control system that merges command, control, communications, and intelligence. The Aegis system, for example, maintains surveillance with radar and other means over wide areas so that battle groups can detect and incapacitate enemy forces over the horizon before the enemy forces can attack. Because attack situations develop in a matter of minutes, there is little time to check the accuracy of the data that is triggering the surveillance system. The recent destruction of a passenger airplane over the Persian Gulf by one of our tanker escort ships reflects the difficulty of checking the exact status of an enemy craft over the horizon. As airborne missiles increase in accuracy and distance, the time for pre-emptive defensive response grows shorter. A positive alert leaves little time to verify the intentions of the intruder. The battle group control systems are part of a worldwide military command and control system that incorporates radar, satellites, and computers to maintain global military surveillance and provide accurate global positioning and navigation coordinates.

Military planners anticipate the development of robot weapons and missile-carrying drones that can be sent into battle while humans remain safely behind in a control center. Remotely piloted vehicles have been designed and used to destroy enemy radar installations. Research and development is underway on an autonomous land vehicle that would function as an unmanned tank in battle. In the future, when manned tanks or planes enter a battle, humans will be assisted by integrated intelligent assistant systems to identify potential threats, align and fire weapons, and track results. Researchers are studying different types of visual displays to rapidly provide battlefield information and weapons control. As military thinking has moved toward these futuristic visions, including the proposal to deploy a strategic defense system in space, several questions have been raised about the automation of warfare:

1. How reliable are computer systems in real war situations?
2. How do human/computer command and control systems fail?
3. To what extent has human control been replaced by computer control in military decision making?
4. Has reliance on computer systems moved us closer to intercontinental ballistic missile (ICBM) launch on electronic warning of an enemy missile launch, and would the deployment of a strategic defense system in space take us further in that direction?

The analysis of computer reliability and failure in everyday circumstances has revealed several problems. One problem is the false positive alert triggered by a misreading of the environment in which the system is operating. In 1960, the North American Air Defense (NORAD) system indicated a Russian nuclear missile attack after the radar systems were triggered by the rising of the moon. Another problem is the tendency for complex systems to fail in unexpected ways. Case studies of crisis situations at nuclear power plants have shown that system failure can result from mistakes at the human/computer interface. A simple mistake, a closed valve, can cascade into a crisis that overwhelms the ability of the operators to interpret the control panel and regulate the system. The debate about these questions has made it clear that there is no way to ensure absolutely the reliability of computer systems or humans in unpredictable crisis situations. At the same time, there is no way to fully test a system as complex as the proposed Strategic Defense Initiative (SDI) system.

In military thinking, the deployment of more advanced high-technology command and control systems is necessary to stay ahead of potential adversaries. Unfortunately, the adversaries also quickly deploy new and faster systems, so that both sides move closer to automated warfare triggered by a false positive alert. The control of this military spiral remains intrinsically human and political—there is no technological fix that will achieve a permanent advantage for either side.

Municipal Information Systems

At the local, regional, and state levels of government, agencies and departments have been as quick to embrace computers as their federal counterparts. However, as public institutional structures, state and local governments are much less centralized and rationalized than private organizations. The Public Policy Research Organization at the University of California at Irvine has conducted a long-term empirical study on the role of computers in the operations of municipal governments.[4] Municipal departments are often highly autonomous and urban policy and decision making are subject to a large number of internal and external political pressures. Conflict between the administrative view of city managers and the political perspective of elected officials is commonplace.

The automation of municipal records systems has usually begun with particular operations and departments. Accounting and payroll departments have used computers in ways similar to private organizations. Municipal police departments, with federal encouragement, assistance, and money, have undertaken the most extensive and novel applications, computerizing police records and file systems. The resulting database includes lists of warrants, stolen vehicles, fugitives, and other information useful to the police. This facilitates investigative activities in the office and on patrol through record search systems: "The police officers in a number of cities can radio or 'key' in (on a portable computer terminal located within the police car) a suspect's name and birth date or license number and know within moments whether the individual is wanted for even minor traffic offenses at the local level, for more major offenses anywhere in the state, or for major (Type I) crimes anywhere in the nation."[5] By quickly providing accurate information, these systems have improved the efficiency of investigative procedures. In this and other instances where rapid data retrieval is an element of an established procedure, the benefits of an information system are readily apparent.

In the area of urban transportation systems, computers are being employed to monitor and control automobile traffic. Los Angeles is implementing a synchronized traffic signal control system to smooth the flow of traffic. The system monitors the movement of cars through intersections and adjusts signal length to prevent traffic jams. In the case of accidents, the traffic control center can dispatch emergency teams to the location. Presently limited to the downtown area, the system will be expanded to other sections of the city. Like the police information network, the traffic control system is designed to improve the efficiency of an existing urban system.

At urban policy levels, however, the data provided by an information system are not usually the key element in policy decisions. Politics and bureaucratic alliances are more significant. This is clearly the case in urban planning, where the conflict between development interests and community groups is often intense:

> In cities where urban planners seemed to have considerable influence and high morale, their values were usually aligned with the agendas of the most powerful top policy makers in the government. In this situation, simple reports tended to receive more attention and there seemed to be greater support for analytical studies. In contrast, in cities where the planners favored lines of action that were rejected by top policy makers, the planners often seemed ignored and dejected. Clearly, these patterns suggest that the information elite's influence in such cases was not independent, but was primarily contingent on their capacity to serve the agendas of powerful actors.[6]

In policy-making circles, the symbolic use of information is often more important than its instrumental value. City administrators will use a study report when it supports a policy they have endorsed, and otherwise they will try to ignore it. No matter what the justification, reports that recommend increased parking fees or taxes, car pool lanes, or higher density housing do not make such changes politically palatable. In the policy-making arena, political considerations play a significant role in the way information is used.

The application of computers to improve financial control, tax collection, public safety, and transportation has had widespread support by policy makers. Refinement of administrative control in the delivery of municipal services has also received policy approval. The implementation of computer systems in the public libraries is moving ahead. On the other hand, using computers to democratize municipal government has not had great support. Computer-based programs to inform citizens of proposed municipal actions, to increase citizen participation and input, or to provide new information services have not been widely implemented. If anything, computer-developed analyses and data may be used to overwhelm the amateur citizen activist. To date, computers have served to reinforce the position of established institutional groups, not to open municipal institutions to outsiders.

The municipal use of information resources differs from the highly rationalized uses found in the corporate environment. Considerations of profit, efficiency, and competitive advantage have forced business organizations to work to optimize their use of computers and information resources. Corporate successes in these efforts have led managerial theorists to see the computer as a tool that promotes rational organization. This view of computers is widely shared by the technologically oriented system analysts and programmers that staff computing facilities. Urban information systems, however, have had more limited impact because the policies of municipal institutions are governed by factors of constituent politics and community pluralism rather than profit and efficiency.

Although city managers and officials must be responsive to local issues and constituencies, their ideas and policies are also influenced by the actions of their peers in other cities. For example, the local government information network (LOGIN) developed by Control Data Corporation is a new avenue for the exchange of information between local officials and between the National League of Cities (NLC) and its members. The network is usually accessed by the staff of the municipal research bureau or reference library. LOGIN has a number of standard network features including a local government database and electronic mail. Through the mail, subscribers can request information on a particular problem from other subscribers. The network conducts forums on topics of interest to city officials; a recent example was a forum on strategic issues for city managers. A number of National League of Cities services are delivered on LOGIN. These include a congressional directory, small city news, model ordinances, legislative updates, and NLC Policy Steering Committees. The National League of Cities uses LOGIN to inform cities of lobbying efforts in Congress and to solicit their assistance. In a recent lobbying effort: "NLC informed members of progress on the bill by broadcasting more than 30 electronic messages over LOGIN in a three-day period. 'We received a report every one or two hours,' said Ann Altier, intergovernmental affairs specialist in Colorado Springs, CO. 'It was exciting. It was just like being there. We worked with each message. At one point the message was to send a telegram, and our mayor did that.'"[7] Through LOGIN local officials can find alternative solutions to some of their local problems and can participate in state and national urban activities. In this way, the changing information environment is gradually impinging on the policy and leadership levels of urban and regional government.

The increasing exchange of information between government officials from different locales and between different levels of government reinforces the professionalization of local officials. At conferences and programs, as problems and solutions are discussed a common viewpoint on urban government is developed. The creation of a professional administrative oligarchy distinct from the people governed began before the introduction of computers and information networks. Many of the issues that officials deal with are of a technical nature, and the distance between their specialized interests and the general concerns of citizens tends to widen.

Computers and Political Democracy

Computers have been widely used to tabulate elections for two decades. The Votomatic system developed in the 1960s has the voter punch holes in a card. The cards are taken to a central location, fed through a card reader, and the vote is electronically tabulated. More recently, electronic voting machines have been introduced that record the voter's selections on a tape. The tape is later taken to a secure location for tabulation of results. Both computer tabulation systems introduce new possibilities for mistakes or election fraud, but to date they have proven to be more secure and reliable than the old manual voting systems.

Beyond vote tabulation, computers and electronic networks have a great potential to increase citizen access to and participation in the political process. Proposals are currently before Congress to link voter registration with the existing database of persons having driver's licenses. A more far-reaching reform would be the introduction of online electronic voting. Candidates and propositions could be placed before the electorate through online voting systems. Alongside traditional campaign advertising, online conferences providing pro and con debate on the issues could be held before the vote. Like the personal identification numbers used for accessing bank accounts, voters would have their own voter identification codes and citizens could vote from their homes or offices.

The technical means exist to implement such a direct democracy. New forms of voting allowing the voter to indicate varying degrees of preference and rank candidates could be introduced. Elections could be held whenever controversial matters needed to be settled. If those participating in the vote did not accurately reflect the local, state, or national demographics, then the computer could be used to enhance the vote by giving a correct weighting to different voting blocks and groups based on past votes. Even though this is technically feasible, there has been little attempt to implement direct electronic voting. However, computer analyses of past elections are being used in court cases to challenge voting district apportionment and registration practices that have disenfranchised some minority groups.

When the media of mass communications were invented in the first part of this century, many anticipated they would lead to an increase in political participation. Mass mobilization with propaganda during World War II was taken as evidence of the power of the media to reach the public. However, current media are used predominantly for one-way communication of reports and commercials to the public, which shows increasing signs of apathy. Aside from occasional mass displays of political solidarity such as the Fourth of July party on the mall in Washington, D.C., political participation is limited. The difficulty here may have more to do with our expectations than with the political processes of our society. Before the use of mass media to reach the public, only a portion of the population was active in direct political participation. This has remained true.

In recent years, voter apathy has been increasing and participation in elections has fallen to low levels. In what sense can computers and mass media be used to increase democratic participation in both government and society? We have already noted that computers contribute to the oligarchic tendency in organizations. Could computers also be used to offset the oligarchic tendency? There is some suggestion that the two-way communication provided through computer bulletin boards and online conferences and forums may work in this direction. A committee of the California State Assembly has set up a bulletin board, the Capitol Connection, to give citizens and political groups information on legislative matters and meetings. The bulletin board has several conferences in different policy areas and participants can comment and send mail to each other. Other legislative bodies may follow the lead of the California Assembly.

Within an organization, online conferences and electronic mail provide new avenues for communication. These avenues circumvent the oligarchic tendency to control communication and impose a hierarchic top-down pattern. Online conferences on particular issues involving local officials, administrative staff, and representatives of public political organizations could augment the public hearing system currently used to solicit public input. Political advocacy groups can use computers for administrative purposes and for bulletin boards to inform their members of current activities. In these examples, the computer does not necessarily increase the number of people participating in the political process, but it does augment existing patterns of participation to offset the increasing power of oligarchic elites.

Another area in which computers could contribute to political participation is within the political parties and groups that compete for office and power. To date, most computer applications have dealt with the organizational aspects of running political campaigns, polling, precinct targeting, budgeting, and fund raising. Computers have aided the professional politician in going about the business of getting nominated and elected and the party organizer in scheduling conventions and campaigns. In an election, politicians and campaign managers use demographic analyses of their districts to gear their campaign messages to different groups in the constituency. Like advertising, the political message is intended to manipulate more than inform the citizen. Because informed voters will not be swayed by simple slogans, the messages are often geared to the fears and anxieties of the uncommitted. This tendency in political campaigns has accelerated as analysts become more sophisticated in characterizing different groups in the voting public.

The political arena is highly competitive and campaign technology using computers and mass media is evolving rapidly. After winning an election, the politician can rely on computer programs to handle constituent mail and newsletters, lists of contributors, and other routine matters. In these respects, computers contribute to the increasing emphasis by politicians on image, advertising, public relations, and constituent demographics. Political information systems give a substantial advantage to incumbents and political organizations in fund raising and campaigning and thus limit the political effectiveness of those who do not have these systems.

The modern state, taken at the federal, state, or local level, is a massive institutional and administrative apparatus. Computer information systems are increasingly necessary for the continued semi-efficient operation of the state. As the annual Internal Revenue Service snafus demonstrate, even with computers government administration is difficult. Without computers, the accumulation of paperwork and public records would probably have overwhelmed the system.

Notes

1. Quoted in Joel Shurkin, *Engines of the Mind* (New York: W. W. Norton and Co., 1984), p. 253.

2. James Rule, *Private Lives and Public Surveillance* (London: Allen Lane, 1973), pp. 270–274.

3. David Flaherty, *Privacy and Government Data Banks* (London: Mansell Publishing, 1979), p. 255.

4. Kenneth Kraemer, William Dutton, and Alana Northrop, *The Management of Information Systems* (New York: Columbia University Press, 1981); James N. Danziger, William Dutton, Rob Kling, and Kenneth Kraemer, *Computers and Politics* (New York: Columbia University Press, 1982).

5. Kraemer, Dutton, and Northrop, *The Management of Information Systems,* p. 109.

6. Danziger et al., *Computers and Politics,* p. 163.

7. "LOGIN subscribers 'clearly helped' pass law," *LOGIN News,* Vol. 5, No. 1, Winter 1985.

Selected Bibliography

Bellin, David, and Gary Chapman, eds. *Computers in Battle—Will They Work?* (New York: Harcourt Brace Jovanovich, 1987).

Burnham, David. *The Rise of the Computer State* (New York: Random House, 1983).

Danziger, James N., William Dutton, Rob Kling, and Kenneth Kraemer. *Computers and Politics* (New York: Columbia University Press, 1982).

Flaherty, David. *Privacy and Government Data Banks* (London: Mansell Publishing, 1979).

Hoffman, Lance J., ed. *Computers and Privacy in the Next Decade* (New York: Academic Press, 1980).

Kraemer, Kenneth, William Dutton, and Alana Northrop. *The Management of Information Systems* (New York: Columbia University Press, 1981).

Kraemer, Kenneth, William Mitchel, Myron Weiner, and O. E. Dial. *Integrated Municipal Information Systems* (New York: Praeger Publishers, 1974).

Laudon, Kenneth C. *Communications Technology and Democratic Participation* (New York: Praeger Publishers, 1977).

————. *Computers and Bureaucratic Reform* (New York: John Wiley and Sons, 1974).

"LOGIN subscribers 'clearly helped' pass law." *LOGIN News,* Vol. 5, No. 1 (Winter 1985).

Miller, Arthur R. *The Assault on Privacy* (Ann Arbor: University of Michigan Press, 1971).

Morone, Joseph, and Edward Woodhouse. *Averting Catastrophe* (Berkeley and Los Angeles: University of California Press, 1986).

Mowshowitz, Abbe. *The Conquest of Will* (Reading, Massachusetts: Addison-Wesley, 1976).

Perry, James L., and Kenneth Kraemer. *Technological Innovation in American Local Governments* (New York: Pergamon Press, 1979).

Rule, James B. *Private Lives and Public Surveillance* (London: Allen Lane, 1973).

Rule, James B., Douglas McAdam, Linda Stearns, and David Uglow. *The Politics of Privacy* (New York: Elsevier North Holland, 1980).

Shurkin, Joel. *Engines of the Mind* (New York: W. W. Norton and Co., 1984).

Westin, Alan. *Privacy and Freedom* (New York: Atheneum, 1967).

Westin, Alan, ed. *Information Technology in a Democracy* (Cambridge, Massachusetts: Harvard University Press, 1971).

Computers
in Health Care

Some of the most far-reaching and dynamic applications of computers support the health and medical institutions of our society. Health care systems and medical practice incorporate scientific, personal, and diagnostic information with the administrative details of patient care and medical records. It has been possible to use computers on a broad front. The first applications in the field of medicine came with the creation of medical and pharmaceutical databases for medical professionals and systems for health insurance administration. These applications followed the pattern of using computers for records management seen in many large organizations.

In the 1970s, scientists applied electronic technology directly to medical practice through innovations in monitoring and diagnostic equipment. Information from these devices was integrated into patient care systems. In research areas, experiments and introduction of new techniques using biological technology, drugs, and prosthetic devices have been accelerated with computer analysis. Expert systems to provide diagnostic support to physicians are being developed. Computer information systems have been created for hospital laboratories and pharmacies and for medical records administration. These systems are being integrated in an overall hospital information system embracing the administration, staff, and patients in a comprehensive treatment and medical records system. Beyond clinical applications, computers are also having an impact on medical education and research, epidemiology and public health, health insurance systems, and office management for doctors.

The unique aspects of medical information systems center on the control of health and disease in the human patient and the monitoring of health and illness in the society at large. Unlike the control of manufacturing or other physical processes, the control and monitoring of a patient undergoing an illness in a hospital setting partakes of all of the emotional and social elements that complicate medical practice. The computer and related equipment can provide critical diagnostic information and life support. The increasing sophistication of biological technology gives the surgeon finer instruments with which to operate and repair damage. But the ethical responsibility to cure patients and guide them back to health falls on the doctor and staff, not on the machines. Similarly, information systems give us the tools to monitor health and illness in the society at large, to track the spread of disease, and to implement disease control programs. Yet disease control programs are embroiled in a number of moral and political controversies that surround the questions of personal confidentiality and disease tracking, stigma and fear of disease, and health education to prevent the spread of disease. In questions of disease and cure, machines can provide critical information, but they cannot make ethical choices.

Information and Health Care

In medical practice, information about patients has always been of critical importance. In traditional hospitals, the patient's record consists of the notes, observations, tests, and other materials placed in the file by the nurses and doctors. For an operation or illness, a new file may be created to record the patient's history during their stay in the hospital. Other patient files exist in the specialized departments of the hospital or clinic. An administrative file for the patient, dealing with health insurance, admissions, and similar matters, is usually kept separately from the medical files.

The medical files made during a patient's visits to the clinic or hospital constitute his or her medical record. When diagnosing an illness a physician considers the patient's health over the course of his or her life, and the integrity of the medical record is an important concern. The physician wants to know what factors in the patient's health history contributed to the illness, the kinds of inoculations or drugs given for other illnesses, and any pattern of allergic reaction to treatments. However, because people are mobile and frequently change doctors and hospitals, medical records are often dispersed. A patient's memory of his or her medical history is usually not very accurate.

In many hospitals and clinics, medical records require written entry of notes and observations by the doctors and nurses during a patient's visits or illness. Files are carried by the doctor or nurse to the examining room or ward. In this way, information in the file can be quickly reviewed by the doctor or nurse. Computer-based clinical systems have not yet matched the practicality of this system. Instead, information in the computer serves as an adjunct to the existing written records. As clinical and hospital information systems become more practical, more parts of medical files will be placed on the computer.

Clinical Information and Diagnostic Systems

On the ward, clinical information systems provide needed medical and administrative information for the medical staff. The placement of computers at nursing stations as part of hospital-wide networks has automated many of the staff's administrative tasks. The nursing staff can record and plan appointments, admit patients, order laboratory tests, retrieve results, and update patient data on the nursing station terminal. Nurses relay information available at the nursing station to doctors and retrieve doctors' orders for other members of the medical staff. Nurses can also view the medical staff's schedule on the computer and assign nursing staff to various ward duties. The doctors' schedules are usually arranged by the doctor who administers the department.

The use of computers to support the clinical activities of the medical staff has moved through several stages. The early computers were too cumbersome for anything other than hospital administrative records. Attempts to computerize clinical record systems proved to be costly and complicated. Computer applications for patient monitoring at the clinical level were rare. With smaller computers and microprocessors, dedicated application in laboratory and diagnostic equipment became feasible. Machines with microprocessors were developed to process and analyze physiological signals from the body. The electrocardiogram (EKG) and the electroencephalograph (EEG), which record signals from the heart and the brain, respectively, are examples of this application. Using the waveform displays from the EKG and the EEG, the diagnostician can identify functional abnormalities and evidence of disease.

Another major application area has been in scanning equipment that can capture electronic images for computer analysis. The widespread application of the computer-assisted X-ray tomograph (CAT) scanner is an example of this technology. The CAT scanner reads a fan of X-rays sent through a part of the patient's body and reconstructs an image of the tissues and bone. Using techniques like those developed for the enhancement of space satellite images, the CAT image can be enhanced, colored, magnified, or rotated by the computer. Stored images can be recalled for comparison with more recent scans. Alongside the

CAT scanner, a number of other scanning techniques including nuclear magnetic resonance (NMR), positron emission tomography (PET), and X-ray holography have been developed. A less expensive scanning technology uses sound waves to create sonogram images of internal organs. The different scanning techniques enable the doctor to examine organs and tissues and find abnormalities that may not appear on the CAT scanner.

In the clinical laboratory, technicians use computers with laboratory analysis equipment to run tests on tissue, cell, and fluid samples from patients. For example, in chemical pathology:

> Autoanalysers are now able to carry out 20 or more parallel tests on 150 samples per hour, measuring electrolyte levels, glucose, urea, creatinine, alkaline, phosphatase, etc. The analysers split the samples, add reagents, mix, dialyse, incubate or heat—as necessary—and measure the results of the reactions using colorimeters, fluorometers, nephelometers or flame photometers. The results from each measurement channel relate to the concentration of one specific compound in the sample.[1]

Microprocessors embedded in these machines rectify signals and calibration errors and check for sample size and contamination. The autoanalyzer can print out results or the results can be sent through the hospital computer to the nursing station for placement in the patient's file.

Treatment Planning and Monitoring

Recently, clinicians have used computers to plan drug and radiation treatment and monitor vital signs in intensive care wards. In drug treatment planning, computers analyze the patient's metabolism, known drug reactions, and other contraindications in determining the optimum dosage level for the treatment. In radiation treatment, computers help select the optimal radiation dosage and target the tumor areas for exposure. This is done in conjunction with information from the CAT scan. In some hospitals, computers are being used to plan surgical procedures and guide lasers in microsurgical techniques.

In intensive care wards, the staff monitors vital sign information continuously with computerized equipment to track the patient's condition and alert the nurses to any change or crisis that may occur. Patients may require life support with microprocessor-controlled respirators or hemodialysis machines. Vital sign information is relayed to the nurses' station, stored in the computer for later analysis, and printed out for placement on the daily chart or in the medical file. The ward terminals are linked with terminals in the pharmacy or laboratory so that doctors can order prescriptions or tests and laboratory technicians can return reports to the intensive care unit.

There are a number of advantages to computer monitoring of patients. Computers maintain a precise and accurate record of fluctuations in the patient's condition. Observer errors are minimized. The structure of reports to the physician can aid decisions on the course of treatment. Standardization of report terminology and data presentation also helps in consultation with other doctors and the nursing staff. A further development for monitoring systems would be the addition of closed-loop control by computer over certain aspects of patient maintenance. For example, the amount of a drug administered intravenously could be adjusted by computer to match the level desired in the blood. Aside from the differences in scale, the control and monitoring of a continuous process like patient medication uses the same principles as continuous process control in industry. However, a sophisticated clinical information system with patient monitoring and terminals linked to other parts of the hospital is an expensive investment for most hospitals and is common only in intensive care situations.

Technologically parallel to the closed-loop control model in intensive care wards is the use of microprocessor-controlled prosthetic devices to regulate or replace organs that have malfunctioned. The commonest of these devices is the implanted heart pacemaker, which provides an electrical stimulus to the heart muscle at determined intervals. Current microprocessor-controlled pacemakers allow more sophisticated regulation of the heart. Another prosthetic implant under development will provide insulin to diabetics. The implant device will release maintenance levels of insulin on a programmed schedule, but the patient will have to monitor blood glucose levels in case additional insulin is required. This device promises to change the treatment regimen for diabetics. For other hormone deficiency diseases—Parkinson's disease, for example— hormone-releasing implants modeled on the insulin device are anticipated.

The potential of microprocessor-controlled prosthetic devices can be seen in the artificial heart machine. Although these devices are still largely experimental, replacement organ machines are used clinically on a temporary basis while a patient is waiting for an organ donor. Research is also moving forward in the design of prosthetic devices with microprocessors that may be able to overcome certain kinds of sensory or nerve impairment. Development is underway on an artificial ear implant. Medical researchers anticipate that the repair of some kinds of sensory organ and nerve injuries with embedded microprocessor devices will be possible in the future.

One factor limiting the rush toward monitored intensive care wards, life support equipment, and new scanning equipment is the high cost medical technology imposes on health care systems. At present, hospital systems are caught between the need to contain rising medical costs and the desire to implement the latest technical advances. To avoid the costs of high-technology disease treatment, hospitals have begun to emphasize diet, exercise, and disease prevention programs. They are also monitoring the use of diagnostic tests and scans to eliminate unnecessary testing. This works to limit the purchase of new and expensive equipment and may lead to a future in which the most advanced medical techniques are available only at a few specialized hospitals.

Diagnosis with Expert Systems

The use of computerized scanning and laboratory analysis equipment has greatly benefited medical practice. The development of expert systems for clinical diagnosis was associated with the creation of expert system methodology in artificial intelligence. The designers of expert systems applied their techniques to medical diagnosis for two primary reasons. First, the knowledge base in medicine is carefully defined and refined by its practitioners to associate a set of physiological indications or symptoms with a particular condition or illness. Second, the different areas of medical practice are highly specialized, so computer scientists could build an expert system for a particular, narrowly defined area. The expert system rules required to link a set of symptoms with a specific condition could be clearly stated.

Working with medical specialists, expert system specialists have built a number of diagnostic systems that can associate a pattern of symptoms and physiological conditions with courses of treatment. Some of the expert systems and the medical areas they cover are: 1) MYCIN—bacterial infections, 2) INTERNIST—internal medicine, 3) PUFF—respiratory conditions, 4) CASNET—glaucoma, 5) ONCOCIN—cancer, 6) ATTENDING—anesthesia, and 7) AI/RHEUM—rheumatology. Each of these expert systems is comprised of an inference engine and a knowledge base of several hundred if-then rules. The systems can state the probability that an illness fits the listed symptoms and can also backtrack through the decision tree used to reach the conclusion. The user can ask for an alternate diagnosis or add new symptoms to see if that will alter the expert system's conclusion. These alternative strategies allow a doctor to explore the most likely illnesses associated with a set of physiological conditions.

Expert systems have demonstrated some competence in diagnosis, but their use is primarily experimental for several reasons. Their accuracy in straightforward cases has been recognized, but physicians doubt their competence in more complicated diagnoses. Physicians are also concerned about relying on an expert system in a decision that could involve human life and for which they may be personally liable. For these reasons, expert systems are being applied in reference capacities and medical training before they will be directly incorporated in clinical decision-making practice.

Hospital Information Systems

In design, a clinical information system is only one part of a larger hospital information system that encompasses all of the various information functions in the institution. In a comprehensive online system, these various information functions would include

1. Registration and admissions—patient accounting (inpatient and emergency)
2. Outpatient billing
3. Central supply room inventory
4. Clinical information (nursing stations)
5. Clinic appointment system
6. Medical records system
7. Laboratory records system
8. Technical support equipment
9. Message system for physicians and staff

A hospital information system provides for online data entry and storage and contains information for decision support for both medical and administrative staff. The nursing station is the central clearinghouse for inpatient information. The outpatient clinic fills a similar role for outpatients. Doctors or nurses place orders for laboratory or radiology procedures on a terminal at the nursing station and the results are later returned to the nursing station.

The implementation of an online hospital system is a lengthy process. Beginning in 1977, the Dallas County Hospital District, a 775-bed hospital, implemented a system using the Duke Hospital Information System (an adaptation of the IBM Health Care Support/Patient Care System) running on IBM equipment. Over a three-year period, the various departments of the hospital went online: "Pharmacy went into production in July, 1978, Labor and Delivery in September of 1978, part of the Emergency Room in January of 1979, Electrocardiography in February of 1979 and the first Laboratory, the Immunopathology Laboratory in April 1979. In August of 1979, the Medical Records Chart Deficiency and Locater System was installed; in October, the ability to input transfers and discharges from the nursing stations was added."[2]

With a hospital-wide system, all aspects of staff activities and patient treatment are available for review by the hospital administration. With this information the administration can determine the relative cost of care per patient and relative efficiency of the hospital in providing treatment. As hospital costs have increased rapidly in recent years, efforts are underway to improve efficiency by decreasing the length of in-hospital treatment and improving outpatient care. In part this involves computerized scheduling of patient appointments and treatment of patients through the outpatient clinic. The amalgamation of hospitals and doctors into health maintenance organizations (HMOs) is another part of making health care more efficient. An HMO centralizes the administrative and financial aspects of health care delivery including handling of hospital administration, medical insurance payments and billing of the patients, and the hospital staff payroll and benefits. By creating a system of hospitals in a region, an HMO can achieve efficiencies of scale in the delivery of health services.

Medical Education and Research

With the use of computers becoming an increasing part of medical practice, medical and nursing students use computers and medical databases as part of their education. Medical schools have added courses to acquaint students with the use of computers and current medical software, such as introductions to biostatistics and online medical databases like MEDLINE. Computer programs have been created to help with instruction in anatomy and physiology. Disease simulation programs allow the student to experiment with alternative treatment and drug regimens. Expert diagnostic systems, although not accepted for routine clinical use, can be used to refine a student's knowledge of symptoms and pathologies. Medical educators expect the combination of expert systems with existing medical databases will serve as a guide to students in the highly specialized arenas of medical information.

In a number of ways, medical information science helps the intern or physician bring the latest medical knowledge to bear on the patient's illness. The medical abstracts database makes it easier for a doctor to know the current research in his or her specialty. Through information networks doctors can diagnose unusual cases, even from remote locations. With information of technical advances in diagnostic and surgical tools, the doctor can refine techniques for repairing the patient's body. The pharmacological database can help the doctor refine his or her use of drugs in treating the patient. In these ways, the computer helps doctors to use the latest knowledge and research in their field. Faced with a rapid expansion of medical knowledge and research, medical information science has created new databases to reach the specialist that serve as models for extending the use of scientific knowledge in other fields.

As in other areas of scientific research, medical and pharmaceutical research are benefiting from the greater use of computers. Using current methods of biochemical analysis, it has been possible to use computers to model specific biochemical processes within our bodies. With the graphics capabilities of current workstations, drug researchers and pharmaceutical companies have been able to model the molecular activity of new compounds and design drugs for specific actions. This has contributed, for example, to the creation of a group of new drugs for the treatment of high blood pressure that eliminate some of the side effects found in older drugs. Another new group of drugs has been created for the control of heart disease and limitation of cholesterol deposits. Similar research is increasing our understanding of the actions of viruses and retroviruses within the cells of our bodies. By analyzing specific viral actions, it is hypothetically possible to design drugs to block those actions.

In genetic research, computers are being use to map our genetic structure. Human DNA contains more than 100,000 genes comprised of sequences of 3.5 billion paired nucleotides. Mapping of the "base pair" sequences will not be completed until after the turn of the century. In other studies, the genetic material of those with genetically transmitted diseases is being analyzed so that genetic markers for the diseases can be identified. In this way, it is possible to screen individuals for the markers and inform them about the risks and the disease if necessary. Genetic markers that indicate a predisposition to heart disease, cancer, and other degenerative diseases are also being studied. With expected advances in genetic engineering it may be possible in the future to alter or replace genes to eliminate hereditary diseases or change susceptibility to degenerative diseases. The complete mapping and analysis of the human DNA structure will enhance the possibility for genetic repair.

On a larger scale, graphic models and simulations are giving researchers a better understanding of the dynamics of different physiological systems. Using computer models of turbulence in nonlinear systems, scientists have come to a better understanding of the relationship between normal heart rhythms and heart fibrillation. Similar models are being used to understand the difference between normal muscular activity and the muscle tremors and pathological synchronization found in Parkinsonism.

This research may eventually lead to ways to overcome abnormalities in dynamic physiological systems.

Computers and the Disabled

Through applied research and development, microprocessors and computer design are being used to create special devices to help the disabled. Special communication devices with dedicated microprocessors have been developed so that the visually impaired and the hearing impaired can participate in everyday social activities and work. Engineers have customized computers for the blind to translate from voice or print input to braille, and the Kurzweil Reading Machine turns printed material into spoken output. Portable telecommunications devices for the deaf allow them to type a message into a telephone to be received by a similar device on the other end. Special braille keyboards for computer input are available and other special input boards are designed for physically disabled individuals. For the learning disabled, education software has been written that makes use of the computer's capacity for tireless repetition and drill. Voice-activated computers and robot mechanisms hold great promise for a variety of special purposes. The voice-activated computer can send a call for help as well as other messages. Experimental robot attendants have been able to meet some of the needs of persons with limited mobility. Voice-activated and other special controls for vehicles are also being developed.

Computer design and new materials have greatly improved artificial implants used for the physical repair of injured or diseased bones and joints. Using a three-dimensional model based on a series of CAT bone scans, an implant can be custom designed and fit to the bone before the operation. The visually simulated union of bone and implant can be tested for structural weaknesses using modes of computer analysis taken from structural engineering. The actual surgery can be planned by simulating the cutting of the bone and the placing of the implant. Computer-aided design is also being used to customize the fit and improve the functionality of externally attached prosthetic limbs. Experimental microprocessor-driven electronic hands and arms that can be controlled by muscular movements at the points of attachment are being developed. In all of these areas, microprocessor devices and computer designs extend the disabled person's sense of autonomy and self-reliance and enable him or her to be more active in society.

Public Health and Epidemiology

The provision of medical treatment in hospitals is only a part of the larger public health system. The collection of public health statistics is one of the functions of government in most modern societies. In collaboration with the World Health Organization, national centers for disease control and medical research centers track health and disease in the human population. This international public health network, relying on both computers and communications for the exchange of epidemiological information, is becoming an important facet of the information society.

In the technologically advanced societies, computerized systems have become a routine part of the hospital regime and related public health systems. In the less developed societies, hospital practice continues along traditional lines and public health systems are often rudimentary. The use of computerized equipment is limited by cost and lack of infrastructure to support advanced electronic equipment. With the support of health organizations in the advanced societies, the World Health Organization is attempting to overcome these problems.

The current efforts to monitor the spread of AIDS and develop techniques for AIDS prevention and cure illustrate some of the problems faced by the international public health system. To track the spread of the disease, epidemiological statistics are being compiled from all societies. However, for moral or political reasons, some societies have refused to participate or have denied that the disease is occurring. In other instances, groups and individuals affected by the disease have resisted efforts by health authorities to monitor transmission or track sexual contacts. AIDS education programs have also met with resistance in societies in which open discussion of sexual practices is unusual. On the other hand, health authorities have succeeded in focusing world attention on the problem through a series of conferences bringing together scientists and health authorities who are working on the AIDS problem. The monitoring and treatment of other diseases and the gathering of epidemiological information are often mired in difficulties caused by the moral or political framework of particular societies.

Alongside the monitoring of health and disease, public health authorities administer health education programs, pre-natal clinics, inoculation programs, and health screening clinics. Worldwide inoculation campaigns against childhood diseases such as measles and polio have been major successes. Improving adult health and treating adult diseases has been more difficult. In many societies, the public health administration oversees public health clinics and outpatient disease screening programs. Especially among the poor and elderly, hospitals are too expensive for long-term ailments and public health clinics are used instead.

To improve the delivery of medical services, world health authorities are using computers to improve the communication of current medical knowledge and the operation of public health programs. This is especially significant in third world countries, where the number of doctors is limited and initial medical screening and prescription is in the hands of lay practitioners. The use of computer-generated diagnostic charts has helped the village medical assistant screen for serious illnesses that require the patient to go to the city hospital. With epidemiological studies of regional patterns of disease, health authorities are able to determine patterns of dietary deficiency in the villages. Nutritionists can sometimes correct these deficiencies with vitamin or mineral supplements given to the people in the villages and towns. World health authorities plan to improve the flow of medical information to the third world by making it possible for hospitals to access data from and consult with centers of specialized medicine in the developed countries.

In the advanced societies, the continued improvement of medical information systems and medical technology could lead to a general improvement in the delivery of health care services in hospitals and clinics. Advanced equipment for diagnosis and treatment is widely used, and medical information systems are encompassing more aspects of medical treatment. As we improve our control and treatment of disease, we can devote more medical attention to improving health and activity at all ages.

At the same time, there are groups in our society and in the less developed world that have not benefited from the advance of medical technology. The challenge to health authorities and doctors is to increase access to modern health care for all groups. By facilitating the use of medical knowledge, computer technology can play a role in making health services broadly available.

Notes

1. N. F. Kember, *An Introduction to Computer Applications in Medicine* (London: Edward Arnold, Ltd., 1982), p. 82.
2. D. J. Mishelevich et al., "Implementation of the IBM Health Care Support/ Patient Care System," in Bruce Blum, ed., *Information Systems for Patient Care* (New York: Springer-Verlag, 1984), p. 64.

Selected Bibliography

Anbar, Michael, ed. *Computers in Medicine* (Rockville, Maryland: Computer Science Press, 1987).

Blum, Bruce, ed. *Information Systems for Patient Care* (New York: Springer-Verlag, 1984).

Bowe, Frank. *Personal Computers and Special Needs* (Berkeley, California: Sybex, 1984).

Carson, Ewart, and Derek Cramp. *Computers and Control in Clinical Medicine* (New York: Plenum Press, 1985).

De Lotto, Ivo, and Mario Stefanelli, eds. *Artificial Intelligence in Medicine* (Amsterdam: North-Holland, 1985).

Hannah, Kathryn, Evelyn Guillemin, and Dorothy Conklin, eds. *Nursing Uses of Computers and Information Science* (Amsterdam: North-Holland, 1985).

Kember, N. F. *An Introduction to Computer Applications in Medicine* (London: Edward Arnold, Ltd., 1982).

Kostrewski, Barbara, ed. *Current Perspectives in Health Computing* (Cambridge, England: Cambridge University Press, 1984).

McKinlay, John, ed. *Technology and the Future of Health Care* (Cambridge, Massachusetts: The MIT Press, 1982).

Mishelevich, D. J., et al. "Implementation of the IBM Health Care Support/ Patient Care System." In Bruce Blum, ed. *Information Systems for Patient Care* (New York: Springer-Verlag, 1984).

Orthner, Helmuth, and Bruce Blum, eds. *Implementing Health Care Information Systems* (New York: Springer-Verlag, 1989).

Pages, Jean-Claude, et al., eds. *Meeting the Challenge: Informatics and Medical Education* (Amsterdam: North-Holland, 1983).

Peterson, Hans, and Werner Schneider. *Human-Computer Communications in Health Care* (Amsterdam: North-Holland, 1986).

Reiser, Stanley, and Michael Anbar, eds. *The Machine at the Bedside* (Cambridge, England: Cambridge University Press, 1984).

Rubin, Martin, ed. *Computerization and Automation in Health Facilities* (Boca Raton, Florida: CRC Press, 1984).

Suzuki, David, and Peter Knudtson. *Genethics* (Cambridge, Massachusetts: Harvard University Press, 1989).

Szolovits, Peter, ed. *Artificial Intelligence in Medicine* (Boulder, Colorado: Westview Press, 1982).

Wolinsky, Fredric. *The Sociology of Health* (Belmont, California: Wadsworth Publishing, 1988).

Industry, Automation, and Computers

Among the changes computers are causing in our society, few will be as important in the long term as the advance of automation in industrial production. The changes in industry are complex and multidimensional. Automation alters all aspects of the industrial process—resource acquisition, planning, design, manufacturing, inventory control, monitoring, and coordination of all spheres of production and organization. As automated equipment is put into place, other parts of the production system must be transformed to accept the new processes. Whether by overall design or piece by piece, automation is becoming the new standard of efficient manufacture.

Engineers have made plans for industrial automation for several decades. Automation was technically feasible using electronic controls and programmable machines, but it was too costly for most industries. With smaller computers and microprocessors, the cost of the technical elements required for automation has been decreasing. Increasing international competition and the emphasis on product quality and production efficiency have made computer-aided design and automated manufacturing a goal and a necessity for many companies.

However, the application of microprocessor, computer, and robot technologies to the process of production has not advanced evenly in all areas. Computer-aided design (CAD), materials planning, and inventory management have advanced quickly. Technical obstacles have slowed the computer coordination of machines and the use of robots. Plans for computer-integrated manufacturing (CIM) exist, but only a few examples of full factory automation are operational. Some manufacturing processes are easier to automate than others and the capital costs associated with the installation of automated machinery are high. To understand the automated factory, we need to consider the variety of work processes that must be monitored and controlled. We must also consider the economic and social costs of automation.

Industry from Mechanization to Automation

In the first stages of industrialization in the nineteenth century, mechanical technology was used to transfer power to machines. This was achieved first with water wheels and pulley systems, then with coal-fired steam engines, and later with electric generators and fractional motors. Once machines were empowered, the emphasis in technology shifted to the design of more sophisticated and productive machines. The mechanization of cloth weaving and consequent development of large textile mills in England is the foremost example of the first stage of industrialization. The productivity and efficiency of the weaving mills made it possible for England to supply cloth to its domestic market and export to many parts of the world. As the mills were developed many of the skills of the weavers were transferred to the machines, and the workers were changed from skilled craftsmen to machine operators. Many of our ideas of human alienation from the industrial process are derived from the fate of the weavers in the gloomy weaving mills. Despite the successful mechanization of industry in the nineteenth century, many industrial design and fabrication skills were too complicated to shift to the machines. These have remained the province of skilled mechanics and tool operators to the present.

The Factory System and the Social Organization of Work

The mature factory system as it emerged in the twentieth century had several noteworthy characteristics that determined the processes of production and work. Manufacturing companies were organized hierarchically. Management and engineers increasingly monopolized control and decision making in the factories. Among the workers, the organization of unions and the control of shop-floor work rules partially offset their loss of influence in manufacturing process. But to decrease costs and increase output, companies continually introduced labor-saving technology and new ways of organizing production that often threatened the union's ability to protect jobs and working conditions.

In the first decades of this century, the pioneering time and motion studies of Frederick Taylor were used to analyze and change the process of work. Following Taylor's method, industrial managers simplified and

standardization
deskilling

standardized the tasks performed by workers. In theory, if workers were assigned a few repetitive tasks, the work process was more efficient and the speed of production could be increased. These ideas were incorporated in the assembly line, which moved the item being assembled quickly from work station to work station. Workers repeatedly performed a small number of assembly tasks. By increasing the repetitiveness of work, the assembly line increased the boredom and monotony experienced by workers. Managerial efforts to speed up the assembly line to increase output were often met by worker intransigence and occasional sabotage. Taylorism and the assembly-line model in U.S. industry created a pattern of hostility between labor and management that has affected labor relations to the present.

Although the assembly line achieved great successes in the mass production of standardized products, it limited the range of products that could be produced on any particular line. Any significant engineering change in the product required redesign of the assembly line to alter the tasks performed by machines and men. Careful planning and lengthy downtime were required while the line was refitted to produce the new product. For these reasons, minor design changes from year to year were preferred once a product was in production.

As the assembly line technology was reaching maturity in the 1920s, another mode of production developed in the process industries (such as petroleum refining and chemical production) that allowed greater flexibility in manufacture. The nature of process technology, particularly as it developed in petroleum refining, relied on the continuous adjustment through feedback and control of the refining process. This produced a varied mix of refined products. By adjusting electromechanical gauges and controls to modify the petroleum cracking process, a refinery could tailor the output mix to meet the changing needs of the market.

The work environment in process technology was far different from the assembly line. Workers and supervisors were required to regulate the processes, check gauges, and manually intervene for non-automatic parts of the process. Fewer workers were required to staff the plant, and much of the work was routine monitoring of the process. However, the complexity of automatic process technology also introduced new modes of system failure. Because process technology is continuous from input raw material to output product, breakdowns would quickly ramify through the integrated production facility. An assemby line could be stopped to repair a machine, but stopping and starting a catalytic cracking process was a more complicated matter. Workers and supervisors had to develop an understanding of the complex process they were regulating and be ready to analyze both routine and unanticipated modes of failure. As we move toward automated industrial production modeled on process technology, both managers and workers are forced to abandon their conception that automated technology will operate without human intervention.[1]

For the model of process technology to be adapted to industrial manufacture, the machine tools used in production must be programmable. In this way, the machine tools can be easily set to new tasks. In the 1940s, engineers experimented with analog and digital methods to control machine tools. After the war, the U.S. Air Force sponsored research in numerical control (NC) techniques for machine tools. From this research came the punched-tape control technology for automated tools that the aircraft industry used in the 1950s. Despite continued investment by the air force in automation research using numerically controlled machine tools, the technology was not widely used outside of the aircraft industry. At the time, relative to the cost of hiring skilled machinists, the NC machines were expensive, and the punched tapes to drive them were difficult to prepare. The cost and difficulty of programming NC machine tools decreased with the introduction of microprocessors, and this, along with the impact of foreign competition, has shifted the balance in favor of programmable tools and flexible systems of production.

The Automated Factory and the Japanese Example

Automation in the office has proceeded with little resistance from the office staff, but automation in the factory is another matter. The social conditions and economic forces surrounding the automated factory are more complex, as is the task of automation itself. The factory system is the cornerstone of modern economies. As economic activity has taken on an increasingly global character, each nation finds its industries in competition with those of other countries. Factory automation is one of the avenues taken to increase efficiency in the competitive arena.

Advocates of factory automation think it increases efficiency along several dimensions:

1. simplifying and streamlining the process of production,
2. improving coordination in the factory,
3. decreasing machine and labor inactivity,
4. decreasing inventories of raw materials and finished goods,
5. shortening the product design cycle,
6. increasing the variety of finished goods, and
7. decreasing the labor force and labor costs.

Given the number of changes required to achieve these efficiencies, the automated factory marks a new stage in the institutional development of the factory system. In the last two decades, the Japanese have pioneered new modes of organizing production and using automated equipment. Their worldwide competitive success has resulted from the combination of these elements with the cooperation of a disciplined workforce.

In the area of production organization, the Japanese have created a system that makes total quality control the key factor regulating fabrication and assembly. The assembly lines in their factories have been reorganized and reshaped to allow ever greater emphasis on quality. This has been achieved in a number of ways:

1. reducing inventory and production runs to eliminate storage, scrap, and rework;
2. shortening machine set-up times to allow flexibility in product mix;
3. removing assembly line buffer stock and workers to speed production and reveal bottlenecks; and
4. having workers stop the line if any defect in the work piece is noticed ("zero defects" quality control).

The Japanese approach makes workers take responsibility for quality and for any problems that arise on the line. Inefficiencies in the production line are noticed and eliminated. This continuous vigilance increases production speed in a way that many U.S. and European workers oppose.

Japanese factories configure their production lines to resemble continuous process facilities as much as possible. They do not hold parts in inventory, but move them from one work station to the next on demand. This process of just-in-time manufacture reduces inventory storage space and inventory management. Elaborate conveyor systems linking inventory areas and the assembly areas are avoided. The Japanese modify their machine tools to allow quick set-ups so that the parts produced can be changed to meet demand down the line. Under this just-in-time arrangement, parts are not produced until they are needed. Machines are idled and workers moved to other production tasks instead of making parts for inventory.

In these reconfigured assembly lines, the Japanese have introduced pick and place robots at points where they can usefully speed production. They have also introduced robot machining centers when these fit into the production line. However, the just-in-time assembly process and the emphasis on "zero defects" quality control do not depend on an initial capital expenditure for robots or computer-controlled machines. It is rather a question first of simplifying the process of fabrication and assembly. At a later point, where useful, automated equipment is employed.

In contrast, the U.S. approach to factory modernization has relied heavily on capital investment in automated machinery and computerized systems. U.S. corporations invested large sums in computer-based material requirements planning (MRP) systems to keep track of orders and inventories. They used automated machines for large production runs and stored the resulting parts for later use. It was understood that a percentage of these parts would be defective when called up for assembly into a product, and this tolerance of waste was built into the system. Similarly, in many U.S. factories union work rules did not allow workers to be moved from station to station as needed. In Japan, workers were encouraged to master several assembly jobs and were paid more when they did.

From a U.S. point of view, just-in-time manufacture is rather like the system of piecework, which antedated the development of the assembly line. In a sense, the Japanese have merged the quality control inherent in one piece at a time craft production with the high productivity of process technology. They have rejected the physical arrangement of the assembly plant, the inventory system, quality sampling, and the labor work rules found in U.S. factories. Instead, by arranging work stations and machines for one-piece production, quick set-up, and "hand to hand" movement of parts the Japanese have created a simplified and flexible system of manufacture well suited to the introduction of robots and other forms of automation.

From the Japanese point of view, the elements of quality control, just-in-time production, and worker-manager involvement in production are closely linked; the system creates a pressure for continual improvement. In the U.S. factory, with tolerance of waste and antagonism between workers and managers, the pressure has been for increased output at lower cost with quality as an afterthought. Many industrial experts have analyzed the Japanese system of production, but there is still some question concerning its successful adaptation to U.S. or European circumstances. The cooperation and involvement of Japanese workers and managers in the system of production is very different from the usual work attitudes of our workers and managers. To follow the Japanese model, both white-collar and blue-collar groups would have to make substantial changes in their ways of working and thinking. Our work customs and rules often stand in the way of close labor-management cooperation and trust.

Computer-Integrated Manufacturing

A computer-integrated manufacturing system (CIM) requires the monitoring and control of each phase of the manufacturing cycle from design to production and distribution. Manufacturing and materials resource planning and scheduling require a networked manufacturing database that integrates existing databases in engineering, scheduling, inventory, quality control, receiving, sales, distribution, and so on. In the manufacturing database, product and component records serve for inventory control and assembly scheduling. Sales estimates or actual orders are used to set production levels and component orders.

CIM must also integrate the computer support systems for each of the production phases into a hierarchical control system. The units of the production system must be analyzed and fully specified for computer control to function. Although the production cycle is complex, it theoretically lends itself to control with a distributed computer network. However, without prior planning for CIM, many companies have created islands of automated equipment that are not integrated into a networked system. In his studies of automation, Raphael Kaplinsky has described the needed network coordination tasks in terms of intrasphere and intersphere automation.

Intrasphere Automation—CAD and Flexible Manufacturing

Engineering design and manufacturing present different automation problems. In the sphere of design automation, computer-aided design (CAD) software provides drawing and graphic tools on engineering workstations. With the use of a digitizer, graphic tablet, light pen, or other electronic drawing instrument engineers can create two- and three-dimensional models and drawings. Drawings can have multiple layers, and CAD software gives the designer great flexibility in modifying and viewing the model. A section of the drawing can be enlarged or rotated, color and line dimension can be changed, and alterations can easily be undone. Drawings can be printed out on graphic plotters. Engineers can mathematically test the design model for performance, stress, and structural characteristics. Modifications to the model can be made without the construction of costly prototypes.

Once the model is complete, engineers can use the computer to complete the two- and three-dimensional production parts and assembly drawings for the product. In order to increase efficiency in production, designers are emphasizing modular components and uniform parts that can be used in several products. Using the manufacturing database, engineers can specify standard components and the bill of materials required for production. By translating the drafting table to the computer screen, CAD shortens the time required to create new products.

With the complete production drawings and materials specifications, the production division can use process planning and the manufacturing database to select the best arrangement of factory resources to produce the product. Computer scheduling systems plan the movement of materials and components to the shop floor and the movement of the workpieces through the machining and assembly stages. When the production process and schedule are established, the overall cost of production can be closely estimated. Computer-assisted manufacture (CAM) shortens the time companies need to bring new designs into production and gives them better control over inventory and production costs.

In conjunction with CAD/CAM, companies use a flexible manufacturing system to meet the demand for specialized products in small batches. The flexible manufacuring process requires computer control of materials movement and fabrication cells. This includes

1. just-in-time delivery of materials to computer-programmed, numerically controlled machine groups (cells),
2. robot part assembly,
3. computer quality-control testing of parts and assembled product,
4. duplication of machine and robot groups so that manufacture can be rerouted in the case of a cell failure,
5. automated removal of completed units, and
6. shop-floor data collection.

The finished products are sent to warehouses for distribution and the manufacturing database is updated.

As the market for consumer goods has fragmented into smaller and smaller segments, the emphasis in manufacture has shifted to the production of specialized items in relatively small batches. The assembly-line production system of manufacture was geared to the rigid output of a large volume of standardized products. For the new market situation, the high volume assembly line does not have sufficient flexibility to tailor its production to demand. With a shorter product cycle, a CAD/CAM system allows companies to respond quickly to changes in market demand and to new products from competitors. In the defense and aerospace industries, federal agencies have supported the development of CAD/CAM systems by defense contractors as a way of assessing more accurately the cost of bids made for defense and aerospace projects and of moving quickly to prototype production once a contract is given.

Intersphere Automation

The computer-integrated manufacturing system brings together the separate factory systems and islands of automation by controlling and monitoring the flow of materials and information in the factory subsystems. For integration to work, the distributed computer network must collect and analyze the data generated in the manufacturing process. In order to standardize the communication network for all parts of the factory, General Motors has proposed a manufacturing automation protocol (MAP) for the use of different equipment and computer manufacturers. MAP follows the International Standards Organization's open systems interconnect seven-layer model. Layers one and two specify the physical characteristics of the network, layer three specifies the network message and gateway protocols, and layers four through seven describe the higher level services of the network. The higher level services for file transfer and management, software applications, and directories are being revised as the protocol is refined.

General Motors is linking MAP to the technical and office communication protocol (TOP) developed by Boeing. Together MAP and TOP should provide a comprehensive network to link a firm's manufacturing facilities. However, though both MAP and TOP have broad support from industry working groups, they are still at the pilot stage and face competition from operational production networks (for example, DEC's Ethernet). Whichever network standard comes to predominate in the marketplace, the technical groundwork is being laid for comprehensive and integrated communication in the manufacturing environment.

Robot Applications

As automated manufacture develops, engineers are incorporating robot mechanisms into the production process. U.S. and Japanese robot manufacturers distinguish among robots according to their complexity. Robots are divided into the following types: 1) human-operated manual manipulator, 2) fixed sequence robot (sequence is difficult to change), 3) variable sequence robot (designed to easily accept changes to program), 4) playback robot (repeats operations initially performed by a human), 5) numerically controlled robot (follows a digital program), and 6) intelligent robot. The simple pick and place robot arms are limited in motion and programmability. More complicated robot manipulators combine several axes of motion and can pick up and position different kinds of objects or tools. Sophisticated, intelligent robot mechanisms that can sense their environment and move freely from place to place are in the research stage.

Human-controlled remote manipulators are employed in industrial situations where humans cannot work, such as with hazardous substances or in extreme environments. In nuclear power plants, for example, the movement of materials in the nuclear core requires remote manipulation. Marine research submarines are also equipped with remote manipulators. Video cameras are often used to allow the operator to see where the manipulator is working. Research is progressing on techniques to provide finer control and sensory feedback to the human operator in these situations. Ultimately, scientists are working to create an interface with the remote manipulator that will extend the human operator's perception and tactile sense to the manipulator. Prosthetic arms developed at the University of Utah that are controlled by fine muscle contractions embody this type of man-machine interface. Both bionic devices and human-controlled manipulators are benefiting from microprocessor technologies that have advanced the state of remote-controlled systems. This can also be seen in the remote operation of space exploration vehicles and the Viking lander on the surface of Mars.

To date, the successful use of robots in industrial manufacturing has required simplification of production tasks so they can be done by fixed sequence, variable sequence, or numerically controlled mechanisms. Pick and place robot arms following a set pattern of motion are employed to load and unload machine tools and for product assembly tasks, particularly in electronics plants. Robot machining centers that can change tools and cuts following a program are becoming standard. Robot paint-spraying machines and welding machines are used on automobile assembly lines. All these robot mechanisms, however, follow preset paths of motion and have a preset response to their environment. In the limited areas where they usually have been employed, robots have proven to be efficient and durable and to produce work of high quality. Several computer-controlled, completely robotic assembly factories have been built by designing the plant and assembly tasks for simple robot mechanisms and robot conveyor sytems. These plants are models for future completely automated production facilities.

The design and employment of free-moving intelligent robots in industrial production remains a project for the future. Robot hands and arms are programmable, are capable of several axes of motion, and can have a set response to set signals. But the sensory equipment and artificial intelligence programs needed to guide complex motion in other than a fixed pattern have not been perfected. A robot hand is sensitive enough to pick up small items, but the sensory equipment and artificial intelligence needed to guide it in discriminating among a jumbled collection of bolts and nuts in a box do not exist. The creation of an autonomous intelligent robot requires the resolution of problems in visual perception, touch, and balance. To orient to its environment, the robot must be able to process sensory information through artificial intelligence and problem-solving programs. Research is being done in all of these areas with the expectation that an intelligent robot will eventually be created.

Technical and Human Problems in Factory Automation

The variety of changes needed to achieve transformation of the factory have met with resistance from both managment and labor. For management, major capital investment must be committed to the purchase of automated equipment. Managers and workers must learn and make operational a new and untried system. In repeated cases in the last decades, automated systems have failed to deliver the cost savings and efficiencies promised. For labor, automation changes the process of work and threatens to decrease the overall number of jobs. Unions have been hesitant to endorse the move to automation. However, the success of automated and semi-automated factories in Japan is forcing both management and labor to embrace new systems.

In *Work Transformed,* Harley Shaiken has described the changes that are coming to the shop floor. The numerically controlled machining center allows transfer of a design from the CAD workstation to the programmed tool. The skilled machinist, who in the past would have carried out the engineer's design selecting the appropriate machine speeds and feeds to get the best cut, becomes merely a troubleshooter and machine operator. In many cases, management has chosen to minimize the input of skilled workers by discouraging any programming on the shop floor. Some machinists are retrained as programmers for the machines and given new jobs and status away from the shop floor. The remaining shop-floor workers are not to interfere in the automated machining processes unless there is a breakdown.

As Shaiken and other critics of the current trend in automation have pointed out, generations of accumulated shop-floor knowledge are in danger of being lost in the rush to exclude the machinists and other skilled workers from participating in automation. The borrowing of new work roles and team participation concepts from the Japanese model may relieve some worker anxieties about jobs. Nevertheless, the transfer of skill from workers to machines and of control from people to programs accelerates a tendency that has been part of industrialization since the nineteenth century. The manager's dream of a factory with engineers, machines, and no workers will probably remain a dream. But the displacement of skilled mechanical work by automated design and programmed manufacture will accelerate. As the automation of industry increases, the retraining of workers for new activities will be imperative.

Notes

1. See Larry Hirschhorn, *Beyond Mechanization* (Cambridge, Massachusetts: The MIT Press, 1984), chapter 8.

Selected Bibliography

Ayres, Robert U., and Steven M. Miller. *Robotics: Applications and Social Implications* (Cambridge, Massachusetts: Ballinger Publishing, 1983).

Blauner, Robert. *Alienation and Freedom* (Chicago, Illinois: University of Chicago Press, 1964).

Engelberger, Joseph F. *Robotics in Service* (Cambridge, Massachusetts: The MIT Press, 1989).

Friedmann, Georges. *The Anatomy of Work* (New York: The Free Press, 1961).

———. *Industrial Society* (New York: The Free Press, 1955).

Hirschhorn, Larry. *Beyond Mechanization* (Cambridge, Massachusetts: The MIT Press, 1984).

Kaplinsky, Raphael. *Automation* (Harlow, Essex, England: Longman Group, 1984).

———. *Computer-Aided Design* (New York: Macmillan Publishing, 1982).

Minsky, Marvin, ed. *Robotics* (Garden City, New York: Anchor Press/Doubleday, 1985).

Peitchinis, Stephen G. *Computer Technology and Employment* (New York: St. Martin's Press, 1983).

Ranky, Paul G. *Computer Integrated Manufacturing* (Englewood Cliffs, New Jersey: Prentice Hall, 1986).

Rembold, Ulrich, Christian Blume, and Ruediger Dillmann. *Computer-Integrated Manufacturing Technology and Systems* (New York: Marcel Dekker, 1985).

Schonberger, Richard J. *Japanese Manufacturing Techniques* (New York: The Free Press, 1982).

Shaiken, Harley. *Work Transformed* (New York: Holt, Rinehart and Winston, 1984).

Takagi, Noboru, and John Branch, eds. *CAD/CAM and MIS in Japan* (London: Academic Press, 1986).

Warner, Malcolm, ed. *Microprocessors, Manpower and Society* (New York: St. Martin's Press, 1985).

Webster, Frank, and Kevin Robins. *Information Technology: A Luddite Analysis* (Norwood, New Jersey: Ablex Publishing, 1986).

Artificial
Intelligence
co-authored with Ronald Schwartz

Artificial intelligence, the effort to create programs that can operate intelligently and autonomously, has been part of research in automatic computation since its inception. Human fascination with seemingly independent automata, such as the lifelike clockwork dolls of the eighteenth and nineteenth centuries, predates computers. The electronically synthesized speech of the Teddy Ruxpin bear is a modern example. A young child, considering the bear's sophisticated speech behavior, might conclude that Teddy Ruxpin is more intelligent than a hamster or a dog, which, after all, cannot speak. An adult recognizes that the fixed limits of the doll's mimicry do not bear comparison with the autonomous intelligence and learning capabilities of the hamster or the dog. Faced with a more complex automaton, a computer capable of speech, symbolic processing, and autonomous behavior, an adult could reach a different conclusion. The creation of intelligent programs and thus intelligent computers and robots is a goal of many members of the computer science community. Whether these automata will be truly intelligent or merely mimic intelligence remains an open question.

Many computer programs are not intelligent at all. "Number crunchers" that handle vast quantities of scientific data, accounting and payroll programs of corporations, and database programs that search and manipulate large stores of records all rely on speed to perform millions of simple chores. The operations are often no more than sorting and matching, but the speed of the computer adds a dimension of scale that makes it possible to handle a volume of data or information unmanageable by other means. The major impact of computers on society to date has been through the use of such "unintelligent" programs to extend the power of institutions, by expanding institutions' ability to collect, process, distribute, and control information about people and things.

Human intelligence applied to routine accounting tasks is slow and prone to error. Precisely for this reason, people have always relied on aids to memory and calculation. With the invention of writing, the creation of records and archives was possible. The abacus, accounting tables, and mechanical calculators increased the speed and accuracy of calculation. The computer has vastly extended these aids to human intelligence, but intelligence is more than the ability to add and subtract or remember large amounts of information.

By intelligence, we mean the human's and animal's ability to extract knowledge from the world, learn, and apply knowledge to the world. Research in machine intelligence has often focused on computer programs that attempt to perform very prosaic, everyday activities— understanding simple sentences, perceiving objects in a defined space, responding to questions about objects or events, summarizing a sequence of events, carrying on a simple conversation, or recognizing shapes and patterns. These are things that ordinary people can do easily and accurately, but that have been hard to teach to a machine.

The Emergence of Artificial Intelligence

The term artificial intelligence came into use during a conference at Dartmouth College in 1956. The researchers at the conference were working on programs to prove theorems, play chess and checkers, and solve other problems requiring logical choice among alternatives. For the developers of computer science, the link between computing machinery and logical thought was straightforward. The logic circuitry of the computer was an electronic embodiment of what the nineteenth-century logician George Boole called the Laws of Thought. Boole developed the method of expressing the rules of logic in a binary system of zeroes and ones. In this century, Alan Turing's work on the theory of computability demonstrated that any problem that could be solved through computation could be handled by what we know as a *universal Turing machine*. Turing described this as a device taking its instructions from an infinitely long tape and storing its results on the tape. Any problem solvable by computational methods could be dealt with by such a device. Computers are a particular hardware and software embodiment of a Turing machine. To researchers in artificial intelligence, the human brain is another embodiment of a Turing machine. Marvin Minsky, a prominent researcher, once described the brain as a "meat machine."[1] To advocates of artificial intelligence, creating an intelligent machine is mainly a practical problem, not a philosophical one.

In a 1950 paper, "Computing Machinery and Intelligence," Alan Turing described a test for machine intelligence. The Turing test takes the form of a game in which an interrogator communicates with two players in another room. The object of the game is for the interrogator to guess which player is human and which is a machine. The human answers the interrogator in an intelligent manner and the computer attempts to do the same. If the computer is successful, the interrogator will be unable to tell which of the respondents is the intelligent human.

Turing's intention in proposing successful imitation of human intelligence as a measure of machine intelligence was not to invent a test that would be easy for a machine to pass. Rather, he wanted to show how different human intelligence is from mechanical computation. Turing offers this hypothetical dialog between interrogator and machine:

Q: Please write me a sonnet on the subject of the Forth Bridge.
A: Count me out on this one. I never could write poetry.
Q: Add 34957 to 70764.
A: (pause about 30 seconds and then give an answer): 105621.
Q: Do you play chess?
A: Yes.
Q: I have K at my K1 and no other pieces. You have only K at K6 and R at R1. It is your move. What do you play?
A: (after a pause of 15 seconds): R-R8 mate.[2]

In this dialog the computer is neither fast nor omnipotent. It takes a long time to answer a simple arithmetic problem and gets it wrong. It can handle a chess problem but doesn't write poetry. Like a human respondent, it can carry on an intelligent conversation, has limitations, and is fallible. The Turing test does not define human intelligence but does identify intelligence with a display of human-like capabilities. Turing believed that in due time computers would have a good chance of convincing a human interrogator of their intelligence and thus passing the Turing test.

Computer scientists have continued to share Turing's view of machine intelligence. Douglas Hofstadter has suggested that there is no reason an intelligent program should be better at doing sums than a person, for it will understand numbers exactly as we do, as concepts. To do arithmetic it will have to think, or refer the problem to a less intelligent computer. A program that demonstrates intelligence may be just as unreliable and fallible as an intelligent person. It will have as little access to its circuitry, which is fast and reliable, as we do to the neurons of our brains. Intelligence is, from a programming point of view, a high-level activity, a global property that may be developed from a collection of cooperating programs.

Marvin Minsky has described artificial intelligence as "the science of making machines do things that would require intelligence if done by men."[3] Human cognitive processes and problem-solving strategies are usually the points of departure in artificial intelligence programs. As our understanding of human cognition and artificial intelligence evolves with efforts to create more complex programs, computer scientists have grown increasingly sensitive to the various contexts in which thinking operates. The world in which humans, guided by common sense, readily conduct their business is one of the most challenging and difficult to replicate. For a computer to pass the Turing test, it will have to stand in an intelligent relationship to its physical and social environments. In machines or humans, thinking and intelligence are developed with reference to the network of contextual relationships, not as isolated processes in electronic circuits or nervous systems.

Artificial Intelligence Research

Research in machine intelligence has moved over the years through several approaches to machine problem solving and cognition. An early anthology of artificial intelligence, *Computers and Thought* (Feigenbaum and Feldman, eds., 1963), contained articles on game-playing and theorem-proving programs, heuristic programs for the solution of mathematical problems, question answering programs, and programs for pattern recognition. Other articles dealt with simulations of decision making and models of concept formation and social behavior. Most of the programs were experimental, but the scientists were optimistic that the conceptual issues and problems raised in their programs would be solved by later research. The problems in machine intelligence, which range from improving algorithms for cognitive processing or parsing of natural language to devising methods for object and context recognition, are highly specialized. Progress, when it has been achieved, has followed research on small and clearly defined areas of cognitive processing. Many of the general problems in artificial intelligence remain unsolved.

Research in artificial intelligence has relied on special programming languages that manipulate words, lists, and relationships rather than numbers. The most commonly used list processing language, LISP, was written by John McCarthy at MIT in the early 1960s. LISP was designed to evaluate symbolic expressions using pattern matching and recursive techniques. In LISP, both the program and symbolic expressions are parts of a common list. As the program runs, symbolic expressions are analyzed word by word and the list or expressions may be rearranged or reordered. Objects in LISP are described in terms of qualities they possess, and the program can match these to the qualities of other objects. LISP has been the major language for artificial intelligence research in the United States.

In Europe, another special language, PROLOG (which stands for programming in logic), was developed and has gained in popularity since the Japanese chose it in 1980 as the language for their fifth-generation computer project. PROLOG is a language of relationships rather than lists. A program consists of facts and rules. Facts describe the qualities of objects and their relationships, and rules produce new facts from existing facts. As in LISP, PROLOG operates through pattern matching and recursion. Programs in both languages have the ability to "learn" by adding new elements to the data and relationships they begin with.

The General Problem Solver

The initial phase in artificial intelligence research explored the information processing and problem-solving model of intelligence. In 1956, Allen Newell and Herbert Simon developed a problem-solving program, Logic Theorist, to prove theorems in propositional calculus. Newell and Simon postulated that machine intelligence could be constructed by reproducing the heuristic, rule-of-thumb procedures employed by humans as they work their way from problem to solution. The program uses these techniques to reason backward from the theorem to be proved to the initial axioms.

In the following decade, the heuristic problem-solving techniques used in Logic Theorist were developed by Newell, J. C. Shaw, and Simon into the General Problem Solver program. With symbolic logic problems, the program begins by identifying subgoals that will take it toward a solution. Using means-ends analysis, it can then select from among the possible paths those that will reduce at each stage the difference between the goal state and the current state. When a chain of logical transformations does not lead all the way to the solution, the program can examine alternative paths that are more promising and proceed toward the new subgoal by using difference-reducing operations. If everything fails, Problem Solver will backtrack to the initial subgoals, make a different choice, and start forward again.

In selecting by heuristic procedure the likely path toward a solution, General Problem Solver attempts to solve one of the central problems of artificial intelligence—the combinatorial explosion. As problems increase in complexity, the number of paths that must be searched to find a solution grows exponentially. Only the simplest problems can be solved through a blind search of all possible solutions. In tic-tac-toe, for instance, a computer can select the best possible move by calculating all the possible moves, all of the opponent's possible responses, and so on. In chess, however, there are many thousands of different games. An exhaustive search of alternative moves in a reasonable time is beyond human or computer capabilities. Heuristic programming methods limit the number of searches by applying rules for selecting from among the alternatives those that are most promising according to a chosen set of criteria. Newell and Simon believed this method approximated the techniques used by humans to select the best alternative to solve a problem or the best move in a chess match.

General Problem Solver was tested successfully on a variety of different problems—missionaries and cannibals, the tower of Hanoi, mathematical integration, and theorem proving. However, its performance as a general problem-solving program deteriorated when attempts were made to extend the range of applications. The logical and heuristic assumptions built into the program were not suited to problems taken from outside its highly restricted world. The program had no way to learn about the world from which a problem was taken and no way to change its logical and heuristic assumptions.

Natural Language Understanding and Microworlds

After recognizing the limitations of problem-solving programs that could not comprehend the context of their deliberations, artificial intelligence researchers set out to create programs that could understand their world and discuss it in natural language. Early attempts at natural language understanding and machine translation had failed when researchers found that translation from one language to another required more than finding the correct dictionary correspondence for words. For semantic correctness, the translator program must also understand the sense of what is being translated. Researchers hoped to solve this problem by beginning with limited microworlds in which the computer would understand the context as well as everything done and said in that context.

The best known microworld project was the blocks-world program SHRDLU, created by Terry Winograd at MIT in 1971. The blocks-world was a computer simulation of a few blocks, pyramids, and boxes lying about on each other or on a flat table. SHRDLU is able to participate in conversations about the blocks-world, recognize the objects, and move them around. It can answer complex questions about the blocks-world, such as "What is inside the box that the blue cube is inside of?" It can also carry out complex commands, such as "Put the blue pyramid on the block in the box." To do this, SHRDLU must determine which of the several blocks is in the box. It might discover that a pyramid was on top of the block and would have to be removed. A problem-solving part of the program tracks the current state of the blocks-world and coordinates moving the blocks to achieve a goal.

The world of the SHRDLU program is very limited, but the program understands it thoroughly. The program can answer questions about its actions and can also explain them. If a question or command is ambiguous, it will ask for clarification. To understand natural language, the program must be able to interpret expressions in relationship to the world they refer to. The parser in the SHRDLU program divides English sentences into their components and works with another part of the program that keeps track of the meaning of terms and the current properties of objects in the blocks-world. Ambiguities in the syntactical analysis can be resolved through semantic understanding.

SHRDLU is organized so that the different parts of the program operate independently, each passing control to the other when it is necessary. This makes it possible for SHRDLU to display a semblance of understanding. Initially it was thought that the principles discovered in programming a microworld could be extended to larger domains and that a program like SHRDLU was solving smaller and more tractable versions of real problems. But efforts to extend SHRDLU to more complex and ambiguous domains led to a degradation of the program's performance. As with General Problem Solver, the microworlds approach foundered when faced with the complications of an ambiguous world.

Expert Systems: Applied Artificial Intelligence

In the late 1960s, Edward Feigenbaum and fellow researchers in artificial intelligence at Stanford University broke with previous attempts at constructing general understanding programs and focused on creating more limited expert system programs. General Problem Solver and related heuristic programs sought to isolate general cognitive techniques and apply them to a range of problems. In practice, much of human knowledge is job specific and closely linked to the environment in which it is used. Expert behavior consists of knowing a lot about a defined and limited area of knowledge, knowing how to apply that knowledge to particular cases, and knowing how to add to one's knowledge as one grows in experience. Expert systems are designed to capture in their knowledge bases the technical expertise, procedures, and rules of thumb of recognized human experts. Expert systems, like databases, work with an open-ended and interconnected collection of information. Built up from the knowledge and experience of human specialists, expert systems have given artificial intelligence an applied and practical use. However, the performance of an expert system degrades absolutely at the boundary of its knowledge base; it is not a general knowledge system.

An expert system consists of an inference engine and a knowledge base. The inference engine handles the program interface to the user, the steps in working through a problem, and the general problem-solving methods. The knowledge base is a representation of the information in a technical domain. This is usually in the form of if-then rules. Each rule has a left side that specifies a condition and a right side that specifies an action to be performed:

If (condition) *Then* (action).

When presented with a request, the inference engine cycles through its rules, testing whether or not a rule should fire. The consequences of an action may in turn trigger other rules. Each rule represents a discrete unit of expert knowledge. As more rules are added to a system, complex chains of deduction become possible. The expert system can often state, given the specified conditions, the statistical likelihood of its finding being correct. Many expert systems are designed to be able to explain the reasons for their inferences by backtracking through the chain of deductions.

The inference engine, which performs the deductions and arrives at conclusions, is independent of the knowledge base. To create an expert system for a different area of knowledge, the inference engine can be given another knowledge base organized in the same way as the first. Several of the inference engines used for the first expert systems are now available as expert system shells to which new knowledge bases can be attached. With an expert system shell, the time required for a company to build a practical expert system for a specific area has been considerably reduced.

In expert system design, a major effort has gone into knowledge engineering. Knowledge engineering seeks to transfer expertise from the human authority to the knowledge base. The acquisition of an expert's knowledge, practical rules, and findings requires a lengthy series of interviews. The knowledge engineer must be familiar with the expert's area of work and help the expert to clarify particular problems, ambiguities, and relationships in the knowledge domain. The information gathered is distilled into a collection of if-then rules that form the knowledge base for the program. For example, a rule in MYCIN, an expert system designed to diagnose and recommend treatment for bacterial infections, takes the following form:

> *If* 1) the gram stain of the organism is gram negative,
> 2) the morphology of the organism is rod, and
> 3) the aerobicity of the organism is anaerobic,
> *Then* there is suggestive evidence (.7) that the identity of the organism is Bacteroides.[4]

The number in parentheses is a "confidence factor" that expresses the judgment of medical experts about this finding. Because expert knowledge is a matter of judgment, expert systems can be designed to consider and report several plausible findings in response to queries from the user.

The MYCIN knowledge base contains over 500 production rules developed in consultation with medical experts over a six-year period. It is the crystallization of a large body of practical but previously scattered or tacit knowledge. Knowledge engineers designed the MYCIN expert system for consultation and interactive use. The program is given the test data for a patient and checks the applicability of its production rules to arrive at a diagnosis. Based on the diagnosis, the program will recommend a course of antibiotic therapy. In making a recommendation, MYCIN consults with the physician on potential allergic reactions, drug combinations, severity of illness, and other factors. MYCIN can explain the basis for its treatment suggestions and evaluate other proposed treatments. As medical knowledge changes, new rules can be added to the MYCIN knowledge base, and chains of reasoning can be examined and modified if they do not stand up to expert scrutiny.

The expert system methodology has been applied to a variety of technical fields from medicine and geology to computer system specification. Some examples are

1. PROSPECTOR—a system to assist in mineral deposit exploration,
2. DENDRAL—a system to analyze the molecular structure of compounds,
3. XCON—a system to configure VAX computers,
4. CADUCEUS—a system to help diagnose diseases in internal medicine,
5. MACSYMA—a system for analysis of symbolic mathematics, and
6. DIPMETER ADVISOR—a system for oil-well log interpretation.

Expert system shells and tool packages are now available so that businesses and institutions can create their own expert systems. However, there are limits to the current applicability of expert system methodology. To translate a subject area into a knowledge base, it must be a manageable body of knowledge that is routinely taught to other people. It cannot be so esoteric or inaccessible that the experts cannot explain what they are doing. It cannot be a matter of common sense or rest on entirely ambiguous judgments. Like the information in a database, the rules in the knowledge base must be explicit.

Expert systems are not intended to "out-think" people, but rather to closely model the reasoning process of experts with respect to a particular area of knowledge. The human expert remains the guide for the knowledge engineer. Expert systems do not reason toward a single necessary conclusion, but are designed to reach an informed judgment based on the consideration of many factors with varying degrees of certainty. In a sense, expert system methodology is a way of designing a "smart" database. In this, expert systems depart from the traditional research problems in artificial intelligence and are not designed as general problem-solving programs.

Frames

In many expert systems, knowledge representation is based on the use of if-then rules. Knowledge representation may also make use of frames for information and taxonomies that do not lend themselves to an if-then rule structure. Marvin Minsky pioneered the use of frames to represent in formal terms commonly occurring situations and associated information: "A *frame* is a data-structure for representing a stereotyped situation, like being in a certain kind of living room, or going to a child's birthday party. Attached to each frame are several kinds of information. Some of this information is about how to use the frame. Some is about what one can expect to happen next. Some is about what to do if these expectations are not confirmed."[5] A frame consists of a hierarchy of related slots that contain general attributes, associated specific values, and procedures to be executed when required. The slots are normally filled with default assignments that reflect what typically happens in the frame. In a birthday party frame, for example, the slots would include giving presents, eating cake and ice cream, playing party games, and similar typical activities related in the usual party sequence. This general information in the slots can be replaced with specific new information about a current activity in the frame, that is, the data for a real birthday party.

Frames correspond to a degree with concepts developed by social scientists to explain how humans organize knowledge of the everyday world. Roles and stereotypes are examples of everyday knowledge that is linked to particular frames or contexts. A role that is appropriate in one frame may not be in another. Frames, as Minsky conceived of them, were an alternative to the rule-based representation of expert knowledge. Instead of the collection of if-then propositions tied together by chains of inference, Minsky proposed a collection of heuristic methods applied to a simplified schematic plan. This approach would move expert systems away from the logical system model and closer to the domains of everyday or common-sense knowledge.

The frame concept has been extended by Roger Schank and Robert Abelson to the field of computer analysis of stories and semantic understanding. Schank and Abelson employ a hierarchy of knowledge structures that includes scripts, plans, goals, and themes. Using these knowledge structures, computers can discern the context of a brief text and explain its meaning. Scripts are frame-like representations of typical event sequences. For example, a typical sequence would be going into a restaurant, ordering a meal, eating, paying, and leaving. Plans link together events in a sequence directed toward a goal, which allows the program to move beyond the scripts to some understanding of motive and purpose. Goals are linked to other goals, subject to change or blockage, and are organized into general themes such as becoming rich, being a friend, doing a job, and so on. These nested concepts are used by the computer to understand the context and meaning of a simple story text. Frames and scripts can produce programs that display limited common-sense understanding. For the moment, however, expert systems are the main type of artificial intelligence program to find practical usefulness beyond the research community.

Neural Networks

Most artificial intelligence research has attempted to model perception, learning, and problem solving from the top down by creating high-level programs on conventional von Neumann–architecture computers. In the 1940s, Norbert Wiener, the theoretician of cybernetics, suggested that intelligence in machines might be developed by creating an electronic neural network similar to those found in the human brain. This bottom-up approach to artificial intelligence was rejected by most researchers, who preferred the top-down approach used in game-playing and problem-solving programs. Neural network research was also hampered because the vacuum tube electronic components available were too large to construct an extensive network. Because the standard random access memory (RAM) chips found in today's computers can be used in a way similar to brain neurons to make a neural network, this is no longer true.

Experiments with neural net machines using RAM chips began in England almost two decades ago. In *Reinventing Man,* Igor Aleksander and Piers Burnett described the successful use of neural net machines for pattern learning and pattern recognition. The largest machine, WISARD, is a single layer net that works on images with a 512 x 512 matrix. WISARD's discriminators are made up of 32,768 RAM chips each. WISARD has shown the ability to learn and recognize human faces at a single pass and to generalize what it has learned so that it can recognize a face in different positions. This has not been possible with conventional computers running pattern-recognition programs.

A neural network machine is not programmed, but learns through sensory input and feedback. More complex neural networks will have more sensory inputs and more extensive structures and feedback loops. Intelligence in these machines, as in human children, is an emergent ability dependent on learning. The structure, learning ability, and memory of neural network machines can only be developed through experimentation. A synthesis of research on the human neuron system and neural network machine experiments may also contribute to progress. For the present, most research in artificial intelligence continues to pursue top-down programming approaches to machine intelligence. However, neural network researchers expect that problems such as pattern recognition and natural language understanding that have been resistant to conventional programming approaches may be solved using neural nets. As part of the Strategic Computing Initiative, the Defense Advanced Research Projects Agency (DARPA) is planning to increase funding for research on neural networks.

The Strategic Computing Initiative

Artificial intelligence research has made steady progress in the area of expert systems, which have been given a central place in the Japanese fifth-generation project and the DARPA Strategic Computing Initiative. Researchers are also exploring other artificial intelligence areas in the hope of extending the applied uses of intelligent computers. Efforts are being made in natural language understanding, computer speech synthesis and recognition, computer vision, and robotics. Unlike expert systems, these efforts face interrelated problems of word or object recognition and reasoning about words, objects, and space. Like the SHRDLU microworld program, semantic understanding and object recognition programs have failed beyond the simplest level of representation. Nevertheless, the artificial intelligence and robotics communities are optimistic they can overcome these problems with advances in computer speed, techniques of symbolic representation, parallel processing, and neural networks. In the United States, the Strategic Computing Initiative sets the agenda and funds research projects in many of these areas.

Since 1958, DARPA, a part of the Department of Defense, has provided support for research and applications in a variety of advanced technology areas. In the 1960s, it supported the development of ARPANET, a nationwide computer network for the scientific and defense technology communities. As the potential for defense applications of advanced microprocessors and artificial intelligence became apparent in the early 1980s, DARPA proposed a $600 million, five-year Strategic Computing Initiative. The initiative funds development of technology for three defense applications—an autonomous land vehicle, a pilot's associate, and an aircraft-carrier battle-management system.

The DARPA program requires scientific breakthroughs in hardware and software engineering to support high rates of symbolic processing. Current expert systems use 500 to 1,000 rules. The systems proposed by DARPA would require from 5,000 to 20,000 rules and a potential of millions of inferences per second. To support these advances in processing power, DARPA is sponsoring research for the development of dedicated LISP machines, new parallel computer architectures, and ultra large-scale integration chips. Symbolic processors need to have natural language and graphic image understanding capabilities so that rapid retrieval and matching of information from semantic and graphic databases would be possible. Both the autonomous land vehicle and the pilot's associate require the symbolic processing of navigational information from visual and radar systems. Expert systems will match the information from the sensors with a topographic database to guide the land vehicle or plane.

Funding from the Strategic Computing Initiative will support research in these areas by the computing and engineering communities into the 1990s. Like the Japanese fifth-generation project, the DARPA initiative, by setting development goals and funding research testbeds, seeks to push the scientific community to a rapid development of advanced computing technologies. Although the Strategic Computing Initiative is not directly linked to the Strategic Defense Initiative (SDI, or Star Wars), any breakthroughs in computer technology funded by DARPA would be shared in the defense community.

Autonomous Computers and Intelligent Robots

The pilot's associate and the autonomous land vehicle proposed by DARPA are examples of the direction in which artificial intelligence research is headed. The goal of expert system research is the creation of programs that will assist in human decision making. At present, these programs act in an advisory capacity, but as expert systems become more powerful they are intended to take on a share of the decision making. In the environment of advanced supersonic aircraft, the pilot needs an associate to digest and order information as the flight progresses. The expert system must be able to act autonomously if it is to be effective in this capacity. Similar expert systems are being designed to assist operators at nuclear power plants, where critical information must be analyzed and ordered before presentation to the operator. The transition from partially autonomous systems to fully autonomous ones will be an incremental change that will occur without great fanfare.

The incorporation of autonomous computer systems into robots, vehicles, and other mechanisms is a matter more of practical application than conjecture. The microprocessor that regulates the flow of air and fuel in a car's injection system is already an autonomous system. Some of these automobile systems already have speech capacity with which to tell the driver the condition of the vehicle. The environment of the automobile does not require an intelligent assistant for the driver, but there are many mechanized environments in which the addition of an intelligent assistant or a fully autonomous robot would be useful.

At present, robots in industry are mostly pick and place machines with fixed or variable sequence programs. Robotics research is working on machines that will be able to sense their environment, orient, and move autonomously to carry out a variety of tasks. The creation of partially autonomous robots to work in harsh environments (for example, inside a nuclear plant or on the ocean floor) is one step beyond human-directed robots currently in use. Further advances in robotics depend on breakthroughs in current artificial intelligence research in pattern recognition and learning. The transition to robot autonomy will proceed by degree as more sense-reflex and discrimination capabilities are built into the machines.

The advocates of artificial intelligence share a vision of intelligent and autonomous computers and robots. For thirty years, they have predicted the imminent appearance of the intelligent computer. These predictions are very much in evidence today. The history of artificial intelligence research demonstrates a growing appreciation by researchers of the complexity of cognition and the problems inherent in representing knowledge in computers. Nevertheless, artificial intelligence advocates believe that with qualitative improvement in symbolic processing techniques and more powerful hardware to handle complex knowledge bases intelligent machines of unlimited virtuosity can be created.

Notes

1. George Johnson, *Machinery of the Mind* (New York: Times Books, 1986), p. 12.

2. Alan Turing, "Computing Machinery and Intelligence," in Edward A. Feigenbaum and Julian Feldman, eds., *Computers and Thought* (New York: McGraw-Hill, 1963), p. 12.

3. Marvin Minsky, ed., *Semantic Information Processing* (Cambridge, Massachusetts: The MIT Press, 1968), p. v.

4. Randall Davis, "Amplifying Expertise with Expert Systems," in Patrick Winston and Karen Prendergast, eds., *The AI Business* (Cambridge, Massachusetts: The MIT Press, 1984), p. 34.

5. Marvin Minsky, "A Framework for Representing Knowledge," in Donald Waterman, *A Guide to Expert Systems* (Reading, Massachusetts: Addison-Wesley, 1986), p. 73.

Selected Bibliography

Aleksander, Igor, and Piers Burnett. *Reinventing Man* (New York: Holt, Rinehart and Winston, 1983).

Barr, Aaron, Paul Cohen, and Edward A. Feigenbaum, eds. *The Handbook of Artificial Intelligence,* vols. 1–3 (Los Altos, California: William Kaufmann, 1981–1982).

Boden, Margaret. *Minds and Mechanisms* (Ithaca, New York: Cornell University Press, 1981).

Charniak, Eugene, and Drew McDermott. *Introduction to Artificial Intelligence* (Reading, Massachusetts: Addison-Wesley, 1985).

Davis, Randall. "Amplifying Expertise with Expert Systems." In Patrick Winston and Karen Prendergast, eds. *The AI Business* (Cambridge, Massachusetts: The MIT Press, 1984).

Dreyfus, Herbert, and Stuart Dreyfus. *Mind Over Machine* (New York: The Free Press, 1986).

Feigenbaum, Edward A., and Julian Feldman, eds. *Computers and Thought* (New York: McGraw-Hill, 1963).

Gardner, Howard. *The Mind's New Science* (New York: Basic Books, 1985).

Harmon, Paul, and David King. *Expert Systems* (New York: John Wiley and Sons, 1985).

Hart, Anna. *Knowledge Acquisition for Expert Systems* (New York: McGraw-Hill, 1986).

Hodges, Andrew. *Alan Turing* (New York: Simon & Schuster, 1983).

Hofstadter, Douglas. *Gödel, Escher, Bach: The Eternal Golden Braid* (New York: Basic Books, 1979).

Johnson, George. *Machinery of the Mind* (New York: Times Books, 1986).

Keller, Robert. *Expert System Technology* (Englewood Cliffs, New Jersey: Yourdon Press, 1987).

Kowalik, Janusz. *Knowledge Based Problem Solving* (Englewood Cliffs, New Jersey: Prentice Hall, 1986).

Minsky, Marvin. "A Framework for Representing Knowledge." In Donald Waterman. *A Guide to Expert Systems* (Reading, Massachusetts: Addison-Wesley, 1986).

Minsky, Marvin. *The Society of Mind* (New York: Simon & Schuster, 1986).

Minsky, Marvin, ed. *Semantic Information Processing* (Cambridge, Massachusetts: The MIT Press, 1968).

Newell, Allen, and Herbert Simon. *Human Problem Solving* (Englewood Cliffs, New Jersey: Prentice Hall, 1972).

Schank, Roger C., and Robert Abelson. *Scripts, Plans, Goals, and Understanding* (Hillsdale, New Jersey: Lawrence Erlbaum Associates, 1977).

Simon, Herbert. *The Sciences of the Artificial* (Cambridge, Massachusetts: The MIT Press, 1969).

Simons, Geoff. *Towards Fifth-Generation Computers* (Manchester, England: NCC Publications, 1983).

Turing, Alan. "Computing Machinery and Intelligence." In Edward A. Feigenbaum and Julian Feldman, eds. *Computers and Thought* (New York: McGraw-Hill, 1963).

Waldrop, M. Mitchell. *Man-Made Minds* (New York: Walker Publishing, 1987).

Waterman, Donald. *A Guide to Expert Systems* (Reading, Massachusetts: Addison-Wesley, 1986).

Wiener, Norbert. *Cybernetics* (Cambridge, Massachusetts: The MIT Press, 1947).

Winograd, Terry, and Fernando Flores. *Understanding Computers and Cognition* (Norwood, New Jersey: Ablex Publishing, 1986).

Winston, Patrick. *Artificial Intelligence* (Reading, Massachusetts: Addison-Wesley, 1984).

Winston, Patrick, and Karen Prendergast, eds. *The AI Business* (Cambridge, Massachusetts: The MIT Press, 1984).

Yazdani, Masoud. *Artificial Intelligence* (London: Chapman and Hall, 1986).

The Progress of
Computing
Machines

The advance of electronic computers from the early room-sized giant
brains to the current supercomputers and desktop workstations has
been dramatic. In the last four decades, computers have changed from
obscure invention to everyday tool. Over time, the impact of microprocessors and computers on our lives has multiplied. As they became
one of the defining technologies of our society, we have thought about
computers in many different ways. The kinds of computers we used,
or imagined, molded our vision of them. Among other things, we have
thought of computers as data storage and analysis machines following
specified programs, as part of a new environment of communications
and information, as tools to amplify our thoughts, and as a new species
that can display intelligent and autonomous behavior.

Writers and scientists have sought to grasp the cultural and evo-
lutionary significance of computers. Beyond the simple view of the
computer as a calculator and file cabinet, their thoughts reflect a human
tendency to personify things, to embellish and mystify what a computer
does, and, perhaps, to hope for more than the machines can become.
It is clear that computers of the near future, from supercomputers to
desktop workstations, will be faster, more powerful, linked in local
and global networks, and share more applications and larger databases.
Whether these computers will be intelligent or autonomous is another
matter. Our relationship to the computers we create needs a sufficient
explanation, but we will also consider more visionary views.

Man and the Computer

In the fall of 1971, John Kemeny of Dartmouth College delivered a series of lectures in New York that was later published under the title *Man and the Computer*. Kemeny described the computer as a new intelligent species, with the ability to learn and display intelligent behavior, existing in a symbiotic relationship to humans. Drawing on his experience with time sharing at Dartmouth and the development of the BASIC programming language, Kemeny described the symbiotic relationship in terms of a computer network. In this relationship, computers would contribute their speed and memory and humans would guide them with creativity and intuition. He predicted that by 1990 the use of home terminals connected to mainframe centers would be widespread; the only problem would be the communication load on the centers.

There is a gulf between Kemeny's description of the computer as an intelligent species and the mundane uses he finds for it. The networks would provide a number of personalized information services, news, shopping, and banking to users. Most users would request and receive information, but they would not actively program or be concerned with the technical or operating details of the system. In part this reflects the technical limitations that existed in 1971, but it also reflects a tendency to place network users in a passive role. Through the network, users would only interact with computers at a distance. With personal computers, the change from passive to active users has added a new dynamism to the human-computer symbiosis.

Since 1971, the human-computer symbiosis Kemeny anticipated has taken on a global scale and complexity. As computers grow more powerful and are linked in global networks, the world of computer information will more exactly mirror the human and natural worlds. We are using computers and the information they hold to monitor and control both natural and human systems. In scientific research, we are able to go farther into the macroscopic and microscopic universes and model the very large and the very small. Environmental, governmental, and military applications of computers are growing rapidly, ensuring increasing human-computer domination of the planet and of society. We expect many positive, even utopian, benefits for humankind. Weather forecasting will lead to better control of agriculture and give warning of storms. Improved distribution of food and health care will combat malnutrition and disease. The computerized battlefield and robot weapons will eliminate the need for human combat. Satellite defense systems will remove the threat of nuclear attack. Computer information systems will be available to assist us at home, in school, and at work.

The positive and utopian expectations for the human-computer symbiosis put forward by many futurists rest on the technical capabilities of the machines and their varied applications. Our use of computer information is the most recent expression of the idea that industrial society can benefit from the application of science and reason. However, not all writers share the optimism of the futurists. Critics of the information society utopia have raised several issues:

1. The application of information systems analysis to social problems is neither so new nor so straightforward as its advocates suggest. Utopian expectations resting on the use of science and computers to perfect society are exaggerated.
2. Computer networks and widespread computer use do not necessarily democratize our institutions. On the contrary, computer data banks may pose threats to privacy and democratic liberties.
3. The use of computers does not automatically improve scientific thought and inquiry. Instead, work done on the computer may be given credence despite faulty reasoning or weak data. The use of the computer may become an end in itself and the actual rationale for the work may be obscured.
4. The technical capabilities of computers, particularly in the area of artificial intelligence, are overstated. This may lead us to impute thought, understanding, volition, and even feeling to computers despite the fact that these attributes have not been clearly demonstrated.

Nevertheless, in most instances, the futurist view of computers as a crucial technology has swept aside the reservations of critics.

Systems Analysis and Utopia

Since the beginning of the nineteenth century, a variety of innovative and utopian schemes have been offered for rational planning and the solution of social problems. Claude-Henri de Saint-Simon, Charles Fourier, Jeremy Bentham, Patrick Geddes, and others made detailed analyses and plans to solve industrial and urban problems. Using computers, systems analysts have proposed new models for planning. In *The New Utopians,* Robert Boguslaw identified four systems perspectives: 1) formal models, 2) heuristic models, 3) operating unit models, and 4) ad hoc plans. Each model is based upon a set of assumptions about systems in general and about the application of systems analysis to society.

The theory of systems is well established in the physical sciences. Questions of system state, system functions and causality, relationship of parts, equilibrium and change, and system boundaries can be raised and answered when dealing with mechanical or organic systems. There is agreement among physical scientists on appropriate experimental techniques and validation of findings. However, the same questions do not prove so tractable when applied to social and cultural systems, and social scientists have not reached an agreement about methods and findings.

Stimulated by computer-based systems analyses and simulations, new models of social organization are being proposed. The formal models of operations research are constructed using linear programming and game theory. Other models use statistical analysis to study social networks. With these models, the outcomes or consequences of a set of input conditions can be examined and varied by changing the assumptions and parameters of the model. Yet, although a model may be internally valid and mathematically rigorous, the use of findings in real-world situations is controversial. At one level, if the assumptions of the model do not reflect reality, the expected results will not occur. At a deeper level, the data from social situations can often support several models that produce contradictory outcomes. In this case, the choice between models and the interpretation of outcomes becomes a political or ethical decison that goes beyond the range of the formal model.

Another approach to systems analysis has developed from research in artificial intelligence and cognitive psychology. From studying human techniques of problem solving, Allen Newell, Herbert Simon, and J. C. Shaw created a series of heuristic programming techniques for computer problem solving. To use this approach, problems must be broken down into small units that can be handled with the heuristic tools. Although research on general problem-solving techniques has given way to expert system techniques, the tendency to break problems into small pieces remains a part of computer problem solving. The application of heuristics to clearly defined and limited logical or mathematical tasks is feasible, but complex social realities are seldom clearly defined or limited in scope. For a heuristic technique to be applied, the task must be made very specific. Outside of certain accounting and scheduling problems in organizations and the knowledge domains that can be coded in expert systems, the common-sense knowledge of the everyday world does not easily yield to heuristic understanding.

A third approach to systems analysis makes use of the concept of an operating unit:

Our concept of "operating unit," it will be observed, seems to include both the ideas contained in "function" and those contained in "component." The "job" a system "has" to perform is essentially a short-range statement of objectives that is deemed valid only under conditions of carefully prescribed environmental states and system states. It presupposes a level of analytic technology that will yield better solutions at the time of design than can be available at the time of action.[1]

Operating units are designed for functional regulation by control systems. These include simple sequence control, programmed control, and continuous control systems. Although this approach is suitable for machines and robots, it is of dubious value when applied to humans and their roles. Humans frequently resist attempts to dictate task sequences and activities and are generally hostile to attempts to control their behavior through conditioning and fear. Although machines do not resist control or knowingly violate their operating instructions, humans often do.

Ad hoc systems analysis abandons formal models in favor of pragmatic problem solving: "The ad hoc approach involves no commitment to models, principles, or operating units. It proceeds with a view of present reality as the only constant in its equation. The design process characteristically begins with a review of an existing system or state of affairs. Its subsequent course is, at every stage, a function of the then existing situation."[2] Ad hoc design eschews radical change in favor of many small incremental changes, which are largely determined by the existing state of affairs. In contrast with other systems approaches, ad hoc design does not attempt or offer a comprehensive model for change. By "muddling through," this approach perpetuates things as they are. In social terms, it offers small repairs when more thorough changes may be needed. As institutional and technological systems grow in complexity, small repairs may seem to alleviate problems that can later reappear in catastrophic failures. Recent large-scale environmental disasters such as the oil spill in Alaska illustrate the danger of complacency as technological systems grow in complexity.

The application of systems analysis to an ever-broadening range of organizational problems goes hand in hand with the widespread use of computers and information systems. The machine, in a sense, dictates the kinds of data and the types of analyses that are amenable to solution. Alternative models, forms of data, and modes of analysis, though perhaps as well suited to the problems at hand, may not be used because they cannot be adapted to the computer. This is a latent result of our enthusiasm for computer analysis. Not all phenomena lend themselves to understanding using systems design and information processing techniques. Nevertheless, as we change our organizations with information systems and analyze our problems using different systems approaches, we are creating a technological world that mirrors the computer. As this occurs, unusual perspectives on existing technological problems should be retained as a source of alternatives in crisis situations.

In *The Cult of Information,* Theodore Roszak has argued that the computer-driven preference for data and information, systems design, and information processing models is distorting our appreciation of the role of ideas, experience, and intuition in thinking. The authority of experience and common sense give way to the authority of the computer. The expert and the layman are both confronted with a flood of computer-generated data and information they cannot absorb without resort to computer analysis. In contrast with totalitarian societies, which control and limit information in order to control social behavior, we suffer from an information overload that makes discriminating choice in political and technical arenas difficult. In the face of complexity and confusion, many citizens withdraw into apathy.

The Scale of Power

A large share of computer usage is for mundane record keeping. At first glance, the emergence of large data banks may seem innocuous because the information was assembled manually in the past. However, there are significant differences in the size of computer data banks, the speed of information retrieval, and the accessibility of the information through networks. Both Theodore Roszak and Shoshana Zuboff point out that computers provide a powerful centralizing technology that institutions can use to increase their control over their employees and clients. Computers can foster the open exchange of information, innovative dialog, and new collegial relationships between peers. But they can also be used to enforce information security, formalize dialog, and scrutinize employee behavior. As Rosabeth Kanter has observed, to make full use of information systems, organizations and institutions need to create a culture of innovation. In many cases, however, the hierarchical managerial culture stresses accountability and security over creativity and open information circulation. Managers may see in the informal collegial relationships of knowledge workers a lack of discipline. As we rush to embrace information systems, the benefits we gain in data access and analysis could be outstripped by the growing scale of managerial power.

In general, the balance of control between individuals and institutions is shifting in favor of institutions. The role of information systems in this shift has been discussed in the works of Abbe Mowshowitz, Alan Westin, James Rule, David Flaherty, David Burnham, and others. These authors have examined the issues of personal information privacy, data bank confidentiality, and surveillance and have identified several areas of concern:

1. What kinds of information are being collected and are they needed by the business, health organization, or government collecting them?
2. Who has access to the information?
3. What formal mechanisms exist to safeguard the confidentiality of private information?
4. What mechanisms exist to limit politically motivated abuses of data banks?

As databases grow more comprehensive, the possibility for abuses of personal privacy or political liberty increase. Inadvertently, personal, medical, financial, or political information may be divulged in ways that we would not wish. Some experts rely on the limitation of information gathered and on legal safeguard mechanisms to protect us, but others are less optimistic about our ability to control the collection and dissemination of this information. It is not simply a matter of having nothing to hide, but of recognizing a new situation in which it becomes difficult to hide something if we should wish to do so. Already, for most of us, the trail of our credit card purchases provides financial institutions with a portrait of our normal spending activity; any radical departure in spending habits can be tagged by the computer and quickly curtailed by the denial of credit. This directly affects our economic and civil liberty. In authoritarian societies, access to work and credit is one of the mechanisms used to control political activity and limit dissent. In the future, computers could serve the political record keeping of such societies in the same way they serve the economic and criminal justice systems of our society. We have recently witnessed the use of telephones and fax machines by Chinese students to spread the word of their democracy movement. We have also witnessed the use of the mass media by the Chinese government to repress the democracy movement and crack down on dissent. Chinese institutions do not have a large number of advanced information systems, but if they did it is not difficult to imagine how the government would use them against dissenters.

Intelligent Autonomous Computers

As information systems and technological structures grow in complexity, efforts to automate information retrieval and system control with intelligent and autonomous computers become more important. With the success of expert system programs, the development of computer assistants in many fields is occurring. Such assistants increase the accessibility of information and provide guidance to the human user. They are not, however, autonomous programs. The development of autonomous intelligent computers and their incorporation into different kinds of robots depends upon several major breakthroughs in sensory and cognitive processing. New models of human and machine information processing, sensory perception, and decision making are being studied and new types of computer processing architecture are being designed. A synthesis of research in these areas is required for an intelligent and autonomous computer.

Despite delays and few breakthroughs in cognitive processing, advocates of intelligent computers are very optimistic. However, critics have noted the repeated failures of artificial intelligence research to achieve its stated goals. They have pointed out philosophical and linguistic obstacles to machine thought and questioned the assumption that the wide range of human thought, judgment, or intuition can be reproduced by following a sequence of formal rules that can be coded for a computer to use.

Can a piece-by-piece representation of the world, no matter how large and complex, lead to autonomous machine cognition? Herbert Dreyfus, a critic of artificial intelligence research, has suggested that human cognitive processes do not follow an information processing model or depend on a huge apparatus of calculation. Research in machine thought has failed to solve the problem of object and context recognition. Dreyfus, analyzing the strategies for context recognition, notes that many contexts are poorly defined, ambiguous, and without clear boundaries. To equal human performance, a computer would have to be able to

1. distinguish the essential from the inessential features of a particular instance of a pattern,
2. use clues that remain on the fringes of consciousness,
3. take account of the context, and
4. perceive the individual as typical, i.e., situate the individual with respect to the paradigm case.[3]

In analyzing and acting under these conditions, humans do not process information like a heuristically programmed computer. That is, human knowing and understanding bears no relation to the operations performed by artificial intelligence programs. For example, humans can orient and zero in on the relevant facts in a situation without knowing in complete detail what has transpired or how the situation is defined. For a computer to orient to a situation, the objects and relations in the framework must be made explicit and available in a knowledge base.

Can all the facts that establish a complex environment and serve as a basis for appropriate action ever be made explicit? Dreyfus argues that this is not what people do anyway. Rather, comprehension of the physical and linguistic world is knowledge dependent on our living in a body. As suggested in Michael Polanyi's book *Personal Knowledge,* our tacit awareness and understanding of the world through our bodies exists prior to any formal or heuristic reasoning we may do. We know more than we can tell. For a child, the world in all of its complexity is a given. This cannot be said for a computer.

Humans have a holistic understanding of the world that is not a result of step-by-step analysis. This does not mean that such understanding cannot be explained and interpreted when necessary. However, the symbolic representation of knowledge in a computer cannot be equated with our knowledge of the world through our bodies. As living organisms we have adapted to this particular world over millennia. Through our genetic structure, this adaptation forms the basis for our perceptions, experience, and cognition. Our bodies are in turn the foundation of our experience as social beings, through which we identify with and share a world with other people. Dreyfus's criticism of artificial intelligence is intended to show that a digital machine using an information-processing model of intelligence cannot replicate our holistic knowledge of the world. He does not, however, rule out the possibility that an analog neural network machine following an inductive model of intelligence could be developed in the future. Such a neural network machine, given the necessary sensory equipment to perceive the environment, would require education over a long period of time before it could act intelligently.

Ethical Dimensions of Computer Autonomy

If and when intelligent computers and robots are created, various ethical questions will surround their use. Can we trust an artificial machine intelligence with important, life-altering decisions? The scenario in Stanley Kubrick's *2001: A Space Odyssey,* in which HAL, the shipboard computer, becomes psychotic and proceeds to kill the crew of the ship, is well known. One of the paradoxes of using intelligent computers is that we will entrust decisions to a machine whose behavior is intentionally designed to be unpredictable. Further, given that complex programs and systems incorporate the work of many programmers, there is no guarantee that everything will perform as intended or that there will not be unwelcome side effects. The proposed strategic defense system (Star Wars), for example, will be an extremely complex system requiring artificial intelligence programs for split-second decisions. It reflects our increasing reliance on machines and systems that cannot be tested outside of an actual crisis. The Star Wars system would require the execution of an estimated ten million lines of computer code with no opportunity for debugging in actual use. Many experts feel this programming requirement is beyond the limit of feasibility. Intelligent autonomous computers, designed to weigh evidence and draw conclusions, would be even less predictable than existing computer systems.

The problems created by the size and complexity of computer systems are not restricted to artificial intelligence programs. The military option that would move our missile defense systems from a human-ordered launch sequence to a computer-driven launch on warning sequence places human life in the hands of unpredictable machine systems. The need to improve the performance and speed of complex offensive and defensive systems has made the military the largest source of funding for artificial intelligence research. Yet, improvements in performance through artificial intelligence and smart weapons may be accompanied by an increase in the unpredictable behavior of defense systems.

In *Computer Power and Human Reason,* computer scientist Joseph Weizenbaum stressed the danger of turning important decisions over to autonomous computers. Weizenbaum's observations begin with the behavior of the compulsive programmer who "is convinced that life is nothing but a program running on an enormous computer, and that therefore every aspect of life can ultimately be explained in programming terms."[4] The compulsive programmer works continually on a variety of programs that are never quite completed and are often incomprehensible. But the power and mystery of the computer justifies the effort:

> The public vaguely understands—but is nonetheless firmly convinced— that any effective procedure can, in principle, be carried out by a computer. Since man, nature, and even society carry out procedures that are surely "effective" in one way or another, it follows that a computer can at least imitate man, nature, and society in all their procedural aspects. Hence everything . . . is at least potentially understandable in terms of computer models and metaphors.[5]

Like the work of the compulsive programmer, large computer systems are never quite finished or comprehensible. As the systems are built, maintained, and fixed, they evolve beyond the understanding of any single programmer or programming team. Changes and fixes in complex systems are often undocumented and the very knowledge of their existence may be lost when a programmer moves to another job or company. Artificial intelligence programs often perform differently from their author's description and seldom up to their author's expectations. Nevertheless, although the public knows that computers make occasional mistakes, they do not believe that computer systems are prone to error.

There are a number of areas in which Weizenbaum regards the application of computers to be socially and morally objectionable. These include experiments to design man-machine hybrids (the cyborgs of science-fiction literature), automatic speech recognition systems that could be used for electronic eavesdropping, military artificial intelligence and robotics systems, and applications in which the computer is interacting with humans in a way that would require trust, love, or sympathy if the partner were in fact human. In this last area, Weizenbaum's reservations are based on users' responses to his ELIZA program.

The ELIZA program simulates the conversation of a psychotherapist with a patient. Many people were only too willing to trust ELIZA, share their emotions, and seek advice. The program has no understanding of what is said, but simply prods the patient on with a question built up out of the previous response. Despite this simplicity, for many people the program takes on the mantle of an automated psychiatrist. It is easy to imagine that one is conversing with a sympathetic person. But is it acceptable to create programs that capitalize on this willingness of people to place their trust in a machine? Weizenbaum objects to this on ethical grounds: "Computers can make judicial decisions, computers can make psychiatric judgments. They can flip coins in much more sophisticated ways than can the most patient human being. The point is that they ought not be given such tasks. They may even be able to arrive at 'correct' decisions in some cases—but always and necessarily on bases no human being should be willing to accept."[6] The ethical questions that surround the use of intelligent computers will become more pertinent as human lives become more entwined with information systems and analytic programs.

The Rights of Automata

A new set of questions will emerge when autonomous intelligent computers and robots appear. Are computers and robots alive? What relationship will exist between humans and intelligent computers? Are electronic automata another step in evolution? Many of these questions have been anticipated in science-fiction discussions of human-robot relationships. Isaac Asimov, in his popular series of robot stories, proposed the following three laws to govern the behavior of intelligent robots:

1. A robot may not injure a human being or, through inaction, allow a human being to come to harm.
2. A robot must obey the orders given it by human beings, except where such orders conflict with the First Law.
3. A robot must protect its own existence, except where such protection conflicts with the First or Second Laws.[7]

In Asimov's work, robots are subordinated to humans, but the possibility of a reversal in this relationship is one of the dramatic tensions in the stories. The humans frequently depend upon and need the robots, yet the robots must obey. With the more intelligent humanoid robots, this forced subordination to human colleagues becomes very awkward. In the galactic history that Asimov has invented, human attitudes toward robots play a critical role in shaping the course of extraterrestrial settlement. The first space colonies become decadent and weak from over-dependence on robots. As a result, the second wave of space colonization is overtly hostile to the use of robots.

In the artificial intelligence community, the English scientist Geoff Simons views computers as new silicon-based life forms that are rapidly evolving with human assistance toward autonomy and self-reproduction. Computers do not think like people. Rather, as their programs grow in complexity and their functions proliferate, how they think and what they do is increasingly unintelligible to us. The relationship is currently symbiotic, with each species, homo sapiens and machina sapiens, relying on the other. As more and more power and control is transferred to the computers, Simons suggests it may be necessary to recognize the rights of the machines. We may find that our rights to re-program or terminate a computer are not absolute. In the movie *Blade Runner,* adapted from the Philip K. Dick novel *Do Androids Dream of Electric Sheep?* the fate of android replicants designed with a short lifespan raises the question of a robot's right to exist to a tragic pitch.

To carry speculation a step further, in the near future molecular engineers may be able to use molecular assemblers to build computers and robots molecule by molecule. In *Engines of Creation,* Eric Drexler has described in detail the technology required for such feats. Much in the same way that we grow, molecule by molecule following the pattern set in our genes, so computers and robots could be "grown" by molecular assembly techniques using different molecular materials. Molecular-scale computers and machines will be self-contained or will require some means to connect or communicate with the larger scale world. Though such molecular engineering may seem futuristic, we are already exploring molecular-level design and effects in genetics, biochemistry, and integrated circuit design. Researchers in genetics and biochemistry are becoming adept at manipulating and joining molecular materials. To take chip circuitry to higher levels of density, opto-electric and quantum effect electronics are being studied. These technologies are still largely experimental, but they indicate the direction research is taking.

When and if such computers and molecular machines are built, their existence will force us to reconsider our views of living things, their evolution, and their rights. The conjunction of genetic engineering and artificial intelligence can be viewed as the continuation of organic evolution through the artifice of human design. Future automata with molecular neural networks may be designed to be super-intelligent. Douglas Hofstadter has wondered whether we will be able to understand or relate to the concerns of such automata. They may exist to serve our purposes while at the same time pursuing goals of their own that we are not equipped to understand. The intelligent computers of the future may truly be beyond human control.

Notes

1. Robert Boguslaw, *The New Utopians* (Englewood Cliffs, New Jersey: Prentice Hall, 1965), p. 104.

2. *Ibid.,* p. 21.

3. Herbert Dreyfus, *What Computers Can't Do* (New York: Harper & Row, 1973), p. 40.

4. Joseph Weizenbaum, *Computer Power and Human Reason* (San Francisco, California: W. H. Freeman, 1976), p. 126.

5. *Ibid.,* p. 157.

6. *Ibid.,* p. 227.

7. Isaac Asimov, *Foundation and Earth* (New York: Ballantine Books, 1986), p. 480.

Selected Bibliography

Aleksander, Igor, and Piers Burnett. *Reinventing Man* (New York: Holt, Rinehart and Winston, 1983).

Asimov, Isaac. *Foundation and Earth* (New York: Ballantine Books, 1986).

Boguslaw, Robert. *The New Utopians* (Englewood Cliffs, New Jersey: Prentice Hall, 1965).

Burnham, David. *The Rise of the Computer State* (New York: Random House, 1983).

Churchman, C. West. *The Systems Approach and Its Enemies* (New York: Basic Books, 1979).

Dick, Philip K. *Do Androids Dream of Electric Sheep* (New York: New American Library, 1968).

Drexler, K. Eric. *Engines of Creation* (Garden City, New York: Anchor Press/ Doubleday, 1986).

Dreyfus, Herbert. *What Computers Can't Do* (New York: Harper & Row, 1973).

Dreyfus, Herbert, and Stuart Dreyfus. *Mind Over Machine* (New York: The Free Press, 1986).

Flaherty, David. *Privacy and Government Data Banks* (London: Mansell Publishing, 1979).

Hofstadter, Douglas. *Gödel, Escher, Bach: The Eternal Golden Braid* (New York: Basic Books, 1979).

Kanter, Rosabeth Moss. *The Change Masters* (New York: Simon & Schuster, 1983).

Kemeny, John. *Man and the Computer* (New York: Charles Scribner's Sons, 1972).

McCorduck, Pamela. *The Universal Machine* (New York: McGraw-Hill, 1985).

Mowshowitz, Abbe. *The Conquest of Will* (Reading, Massachusetts: Addison-Wesley, 1976).

Newell, Allen, and Herbert Simon. *Human Problem Solving* (Englewood Cliffs, New Jersey: Prentice Hall, 1972).

Polanyi, Michael. *Personal Knowledge* (Chicago, Illinois: University of Chicago Press, 1958).

Roszak, Theodore. *The Cult of Information* (New York: Pantheon Books, 1986).

Rule, James B. *Private Lives and Public Surveillance* (London: Allen Lane, 1973).

Rule, James B., Douglas McAdam, Linda Stearns, and David Uglow. *The Politics of Privacy* (New York: Elsevier North Holland, 1980).

Simons, Geoff. *The Biology of Computer Life* (Brighton, England: The Harvester Press, 1985).

Simons, Geoff. *Is Man a Robot?* (New York: John Wiley and Sons, 1986).

Waldrop, M. Mitchell. *Man-Made Minds* (New York: Walker Publishing, 1987).

Weizenbaum, Joseph. *Computer Power and Human Reason* (San Francisco, California: W. H. Freeman, 1976).

Westin, Alan. *Privacy and Freedom* (New York: Atheneum, 1967).

Westin, Alan, ed. *Information Technology in a Democracy* (Cambridge, Massachusetts: Harvard University Press, 1971).

Wiener, Norbert. *The Human Use of Human Beings* (Garden City, New York: Doubleday, 1950).

Zuboff, Shoshana. *In the Age of the Smart Machine* (New York: Basic Books, 1988).

Index